PELICAN BOOKS
A 61

AN INTRODUCTION TO MODERN ARCHITECTURE

J. M. RICHARDS

J. M. Richards was born in 1907, studied architecture at the A.A. School in London, and worked at it afterwards in Canada, the U.S.A., London, and Dublin. But in 1933 he gave up the practice of architecture to become a journalist and critic and was successively assistant editor of the *Architects' Journal* and the *Architectural Review*. During the war he worked for the Ministry of Information, most of the time in the Middle East, where he was Director of Publications. After the war he returned to the *Architectural Review*, of which he is now editor. He is also a frequent broadcaster on sound and television and a member of the Royal Fine Art Commission. He has been Visiting Professor of Architecture at Leeds University and was made a C.B.E. in 1959. Besides many articles on art and architecture in English and foreign periodicals, he has written several other books, including *A Miniature History of the English House*, *The Castles on the Ground*, *The Functional Tradition in Early Industrial Buildings*, and *An Architectural Journey in Japan*; and he has edited a book on *New Buildings in the Commonwealth* and a small guide to modern architecture in Finland.

AN INTRODUCTION TO
MODERN ARCHITECTURE

BY J. M. RICHARDS

PENGUIN BOOKS
BALTIMORE · MARYLAND

Penguin Books Ltd, Harmondsworth, Middlesex, England
Penguin Books Inc., 3300 Clipper Mill Road, Baltimore 11, Md, U.S.A.
Penguin Books Pty Ltd, Ringwood, Victoria, Australia

—

First published 1940
Reprinted 1941, 1944, 1948
Revised and reprinted 1953 and 1956
Reprinted 1959, 1960
Revised edition 1962
Reprinted 1963, 1965

—

Copyright © J. M. Richards, 1940, 1962

—

Made and printed in Great Britain
by Hunt Barnard & Co. Ltd, Aylesbury
Collogravure plates by Harrison & Sons
Set in Monotype Times

CONTENTS

	LIST OF PLATES	6
	ACKNOWLEDGEMENTS	8
I.	INTRODUCTION	9
II.	WHY A 'MODERN' ARCHITECTURE?	16
III.	ARCHITECTURE AND MACHINERY	30
IV.	NEW MATERIALS AND METHODS	45
V.	THE GROWTH OF THE IDEA	61
VI.	AFTER 1918	80
VII.	THE MODERN ARCHITECTURAL SCENE	101
VIII.	SOME MODERN BUILDINGS	126
	BIBLIOGRAPHY	164
	INDEX	173

LIST OF PLATES

1. 1824–8. St Katharine's Docks, London
2. 1859. Red House, Bexley Heath, Kent
3. Top, 1901. The Pastures, North Luffenham, Rutland
   Bottom, 1899. Sitting-room of The Orchard, Chorley Wood
4. 1893. An *Art Nouveau* interior
5. 1898–9. Glasgow School of Art
6. Top, 1851. The Crystal Palace, London
   Bottom, 1889. The *Galerie des Machines*, Paris
7. 1899–1906. Department store, Chicago
8. Top, 1910. House in Vienna
   Bottom, 1901. House at Oak Park, Illinois
9. 1909. A factory in the Huttenstrasse, Berlin
10. 1916. Reinforced concrete hangars at Orly, France
11. Top, 1925. The *Bauhaus* at Dessau, Germany
    Bottom, 1929. Section of Siemensstadt housing scheme, Berlin
12. Top, 1925–6. Reinforced concrete bridge, Valtschiel, Switzerland
    Bottom, 1927. Row of small houses, Stuttgart
13. 1925. Reinforced concrete church, Le Raincy, France
14. Top, 1927. House at Garches, near Paris
    Bottom, 1929–31. Staircase hall of the Villa Savoye, Poissy
15. Top and Bottom, 1930. Stockholm Exhibition
16. 1932. Paimio Tuberculosis Sanatorium, Finland
17. 1932. Elementary school, Villejuif, Paris
18. Top, 1934. Bergpolder flats, Rotterdam
    Bottom, 1936. Flats, Doldertal, Zürich
19. 1934. Old Age Pensions Institute, Prague
20. Left, 1930. *Daily News* building, New York
    Right, 1932. Philadelphia Savings building
21. 1937. Ministry of Education, Rio de Janeiro
22. 1931. Chemical factory, Beeston, Nottinghamshire
23. 1932. Arnos Grove underground station
24. 1935. Highpoint flats, Highgate, London
25. 1936. Bexhill Entertainments Pavilion
26. Top, 1936. Kensal House, Ladbroke Grove, London
    Bottom, 1938. Penguin Pool at the Dudley Zoo
27. Top and Bottom, 1938. All-timber country house, Halland, Sussex

LIST OF PLATES

28. 1938. Electricity showrooms, Regent Street
29. 1936–9. Peter Jones department store, Sloane Square, London
30. 1938. Finsbury Borough Health Centre
31. 1960. Pirelli building, Milan
32. Top, 1950. Railway terminus at Rome
    Bottom, 1951. Civic centre at Säynätsalo, Finland
33. Top, 1940. Crematorium outside Stockholm
    Bottom, 1946. Flats, Grondal, Stockholm
34. Top, 1947–52. Flats at Marseilles
    Bottom, 1955. Chapel at Ronchamp, France
35. 1957. Business training college at Heidelberg, Germany
36. Top, 1939. House at Cohasset, Massachusetts
    Bottom, 1951. Living-room of house at Six Moon Hill, Boston, Massachusetts
37. 1946. House in Colorado
38. 1938. Taliesin West, near Phoenix, Arizona
39. Top, 1947. Opera House, Stockbridge, Massachusetts
    Bottom, 1953. Metals and Minerals Research Building, Chicago
40. 1952. Lever building, New York
41. Top, 1949–54. Residential neighbourhood, Pedregulho, Rio de Janeiro
    Bottom, 1958. President's palace at Brasilia
42. Top and Bottom, 1951. Infants' School, St Albans
43. 1950. Housing in Pimlico, Westminster
44. Left and Right, 1951. South Bank Exhibition
45. 1951. Royal Festival Hall, London
46. 1951. Factory at Brynmawr, South Wales
47. Top, 1953. Secondary school, Cranford, Middlesex
    Bottom, 1954. Offices, Poole, Dorset
48. Left, 1957. Flats at Roehampton, London
    Right, 1958. Gatwick airport, Sussex

ACKNOWLEDGEMENTS

I AM indebted to the Architectual Press for permission to make use of the *Architectural Review*'s fine collection of photographs of modern English buildings. All the English examples in the second and third groups of illustrations, Plates 22–30 and 42–8, are drawn from this collection with the exception of Plate 23, which is lent by London Transport, Plate 29, which is lent by the architects of the building, and Plate 48 (left), lent by the London County Council. Thanks are also due to the Architectural Press for permission to use Plate 34 (bottom). I am indebted to the late P. Morton Shand for Plates 12, 17, 18 (top), and 19; to Dr N. Pevsner for Plates 2, 4, 5, and 9; to the late C. F. A. Voysey for the two photographs of his own work, Plate 3; to Mr G. E. Kidder Smith for Plates 21, 33 (top) and for the photograph which appears on the back cover; to Mr R. Stallard for Plate 34 (top); to the Luce Agency, Rome, for Plate 32 (top); and to the following photographers of the American buildings illustrated: Gottscho-Schleisner, Plates 20 (left) and 39 (top); Paul Davis, Plate 36 (top); Ezra Stoller, Plate 36 (bottom); Julius Shulman, Plate 37; P. E. Guerrero, Plate 38; Hedrich-Blessing, Plate 39 (bottom), and Marcel Gautherot, Plate 40. The line drawing on page 144 is by R. Vaughan.

J. M. R.

CHAPTER I
INTRODUCTION

THE words 'modern architecture' are used here to mean something more particular than contemporary architecture. They are used to mean the new kind of architecture that is growing up with this century as this century's own contribution to the art of architecture; the work of those people, whose number is happily increasing, who understand that architecture is a social art related to the life of the people it serves, not an academic exercise in applied ornament. The question that immediately arises, whether there is in fact enough difference between people's lives as they are lived in this century and as they were lived in previous centuries to justify a truly 'modern' architecture being very different from that of the past – and indeed whether 'modern' architecture is quite as revolutionary as it is supposed to be – must be discussed later.

But there can be no denying that examples of an architecture entirely different from what our fathers were accustomed to have appeared on the scene during the last twenty years, following their appearance in other countries during perhaps twice that period. And there can be no denying that the designers of these buildings are extremely sincere. They are not, as their detractors often suggest, 'Bolshies' or stuntmongers. They have thought things out very thoroughly, and they believe that the new architecture that we are calling 'modern' (henceforward we will drop the quotation marks) is something that is needed in the world today. They believe also that in developing and perfecting it so as to answer this century's problems and to be in tune with its outlook, they are helping at the revival of architecture as a live art – something that even those who find it difficult to admire the form the new architecture is taking admit that it had not been for many years previously. For it is a mistake to suppose that, because modern architects are particularly concerned to relate buildings more closely to the needs they have to serve, they are only interested in the practical side of architecture. They know that they are practising an art, and are therefore concerned with the pursuit of beauty. They feel however that it is time we made clear the difference between beauty itself and the merely conventional forms that habit has made us associate with it. But that also is a question that we must discuss later.

All this, in any case, is what the modern architects themselves think; they have had to fight to get this viewpoint accepted, because it was natural for the man in the street to see in the new architecture only another bewildering addition to the variety of architectural styles already offered him: a new style which, he felt, must have something to it, because it looked clean and efficient and not too pompous and because he had heard that it is based on an idea called functionalism (or 'fitness for purpose') which at least sounded sensible if rather inhuman; but a style that he also rather suspected, simply because he is naturally conservative. He dislikes having something familiar replaced by something unfamiliar without very evident reason, and he had an idea – in fact he still has – that the people who are responsible for the new architecture are cranks, foreigners, revolutionaries, or other kinds of people that he disapproves of.

Nevertheless, modern architecture has been much better understood and appreciated in the last few years, and the purpose of this book is simply to try to enlarge understanding still further by describing to people who do not pretend to know anything about architecture, how these new buildings come to look as they do, why they are different for other reasons than for the sake of being different, and why their designers believe them to be the forerunners of a new architecture of the future.

There have been so many misunderstandings about modern architecture that before we begin to discuss what it is, it may be as well to mention a few things that it is not. It is not, for one thing, a fashionable style of jazz ornament; it is not the custom of building in concrete, or with flat roofs and horizontal window-panes; it is not 'functionalism'. It *is* quite simply, like all good architecture, the honest product of science and art. It aims at once more relating methods of building as closely as possible to real needs. In fact it is nothing more or less than the exact modern equivalent of the architecture that flourished in previous ages, but fell into decay during the last century through architects having got out of touch with life and having forgotten what architecture was really for.

There are several other reasons why it is important just now for the man in the street to understand a little more what modern architecture is all about, besides the reason of satisfying his own curiosity and justifying the architects who produce it. One reason is that, like all movements that contain something new as well as something important, the modern movement in architecture acquired a following of imitators: vulgarizers who joined up with the movement only in order to cash in, as it were, on its news value. To this category belong all the makers of jazz-modern shop fronts in chromium plate and glass, all the purveyors of smart angular furniture and all the builders of nasty 'modernistic' villas; people who have no understanding of modern architecture's ideals, but who could not have come into being without it. This bogus modernism, whether it is the result of the commercial exploitation of novelty or merely the wish to be in the fashion, has done great harm to the cause of good modern architecture by bringing it into disrepute. And the only way to prevent the fine ideals of the one from being vulgarized into insignificance by the other is for people to discriminate better between them. If people understand the point of genuine modern architecture and appreciate what it is trying to do, they will see quickly enough that the ungenuine – which is often called 'modernistic' – has no basis beyond itself. It consists only of a few flashy tricks and the use (often the wrong use) of a number of fashionable materials.

It will be objected that if the real modern architecture represents the revival of architecture as an art, and the bogus modern architecture is only a few flashy tricks, it should be easy enough to tell them apart, because the former will be beautiful and moving – in fact will have the qualities of a work of art – while the latter will appear what it is: trivial and vulgar. One answer is, unfortunately, that we cannot rely on our own good taste. The state of architecture and the design of nearly everything around us has sunk so low that we are no longer capable of judging what is good. We have become so bewildered by the various and meaningless structures that have been put up for a hundred years in the name of architecture, that we have ceased to look at buildings with the eyes with which one should look at a work of art. Instead we have become accustomed to look at the superficial trappings of architecture and admire them or otherwise as ornamentation – and even then not with our eyes but with our minds. We judge them according to a literary standpoint, and only think about whether they look imposing or romantic or antique, or whether they conform correctly to certain 'styles'. Or else we do not look at all, but shrug our shoulders and say that we suppose these architects know what they are about; it is all very mysterious and professional. So one answer is that we simply have not the ability to discriminate about architecture, because we have no real aesthetic standards to judge by. In fact we have no taste, only habits – and generally bad habits. We shall acquire taste only by taking pains to develop our visual sensibility and our knowledge.

Another answer is that in all but a few cases even the best modern architecture has at present only a limited amount of positive appeal to our eyes. It will take time to get used to it; and, moreover, modern architects had at first to spend a large proportion of their energy eradicating the old bad habits from the practice of architecture. Having succeeded in getting away from the imitation of the styles of previous centuries, they were, and are, often content to be severely practical and aesthetically inoffensive. Perhaps, apart from wanting to proceed only one step at a time, they were anxious to begin by emphasizing the aspects of their own architecture that mark it most clearly as different from the kind that went before. For whatever reason, modern architecture has been passing through a sort of 'puritan' phase, in which the negative virtues of simplicity and efficiency have been allowed to dominate, and since 1939 a concentration on the essentials has also been necessitated in most countries by the overriding need to build cheaply. The important thing in the future is that modern architecture should blossom into full maturity without losing the sincerity which is at present its special virtue, or the inevitability which it gets from its appearance being so closely related to its structure. It must not become merely decorative: an imitation of itself.

Although more public understanding of the basis on which modern buildings are designed would make it far easier for a good standard of architecture to be established, it is nevertheless not suggested that good intention should be admitted as an excuse for bad performance, or that knowing how it got like that will make a bad building better. Architecture, besides being a social art, is a visual art, and aesthetic judgement must be independent of intellectual knowledge. But neither will it help to disparage the ideals of modern architecture on account of failings due to immaturity. That would only discourage perseverance.

One of the difficulties in writing this book is going to be that architecture cannot really be treated as a thing by itself. It merges imperceptibly, directly we begin to talk about its place in everyday life, into other subjects like housing, town-planning, transport, even politics (the private ownership of land, for example, is one of the things that make the orderly development of our towns – which constitutes the whole background of architecture – so difficult to achieve). It is also linked up with the other arts and crafts and with garden design and the design of furniture and textiles and all kinds of equipment, and with manufacturing processes. But all these subjects obviously cannot be dealt with in one book. So for our present purpose, although these subjects may be touched on in our arguments, we shall confine ourselves to the discussion of architecture in the sense of the design of separate buildings, although in regarding it thus we risk becoming guilty of the very mistake that modern architects are most careful to avoid; namely, that of dissociating individual buildings from their social setting, and thereby taking for granted things that on analysis we might find to be only conventions. The modern architect makes it part of his creed to accept no predetermined solution to a problem; never to design, that is to say, by rule of thumb, but to decide everything on its own merits.

At the moment we are in a position of questioning many things that we have previously taken for granted. To take one instance, modern town-planners are beginning to understand that it is not on ground of logic but of habit that we live in rows of houses either side of traffic routes, instead of, for example, in groups of houses placed in a park, with the through traffic going independently across country like the railways. In the same way it is probable that the conception of architecture (which is really a Victorian one) as consisting of a large number of unrelated buildings, will have disappeared from the world of the future, and we shall be able to study architecture whole. Today, however, we have but few opportunities of doing more than study scattered samples in the shape of individual buildings. Fuller discussion about the wider aspects of architecture and about the other subjects allied to it can be found in some of the books listed in the Bibliography.

Finally it may be mentioned that in this book it has not been thought necessary to give much space to the condemnation of the stupider architecture of recent years. Presumably all thinking people now agree that it is absurd to put up houses that look like miniature castles, petrol stations that look like medieval barns, and department stores that look like the palaces of Renaissance bishops – quite apart from being extremely inefficient. No arguments are needed against dressing up our buildings in fancy costumes borrowed from the past. A more profitable occupation is to give our undivided attention to the new architecture of the mid twentieth century which is at last evolving.

CHAPTER II

WHY A 'MODERN' ARCHITECTURE?

I SAID in the Introduction that the architects of the last century had got out of touch with life. Perhaps it would be truer to say that it was life that got out of touch with architects. The Victorian age comes in for a lot of abuse, much of it quite justifiable; but the result is a common belief that architects at this time were in some way incapable of producing anything but what was ugly. The best architects of the nineteenth century were, as a matter of fact, men of remarkable ability and enthusiasm who in other circumstances would have been producing fine architecture. They had all the talent necessary. It was the time that had gone wrong. Ideas and habits failed to adapt themselves to a number of revolutionary developments that took place round about the beginning of the century. Architecture got left behind in the march of Progress, and architects found themselves in a wholly artificial position, living and working in an unreal world. Having, for reasons that we shall see, lost touch and confidence, they were driven to look back instead of forward; and what we call their bad taste was simply 'taste' exercised far too independently of the real function of architecture.

In the previous century, the eighteenth, everything was straightforward. Good architecture was the result of keeping to the rules; but that does not mean that good architecture was automatically produced by rule of thumb. It means that the architect's imagination and his artistic sense were exercised within the limits set by a universal architectural language. It does not matter that the particular language in use was one derived from that of an earlier period; that unlike the medieval style of building, which had grown up gradually as a result of centuries of experiment in stone construction, the Renaissance style of the seventeenth and eighteenth centuries was imported ready-made. It was based on the revival of Classical architecture in Italy. But it did not long remain a foreign style. It quickly became adapted to the needs and climates of the different countries in which it took root, and, what is most important, it became the only current style.

'Style' is a confusing word to use, because since the time we are speaking of the practice of indiscriminately reviving past styles has given it quite a different meaning, that of fancy costumes in which buildings may be clothed according to the whim of their designer. But seventeenth- and eighteenth-century architects did not simply copy the past, any more than did medieval architects; and style was something more than a costume into which the carcass of a building had to be forced. They designed their buildings according to the needs of their own day; they thought first of convenience and spaciousness and dignity, and their style was only a natural veneer of manners: a set of conventions corresponding more closely to the accepted conventions of dress than to the assumption of fancy costume. Look at a typical eighteenth-century (what we call a Georgian) house, with its large windows, its regular simple façade, and its convenient commodious plan. It is first and foremost a sensible job of building; at the same time, because the conventions that we call 'style' or architectural language were widespread and well observed, we can rely on its proportions being good. For the same reasons the various ornamental features that the conventions demanded – the ribbons and ruffles, as it were, of its dress – are properly related to the whole, and are not indiscriminately applied but used instead to adorn some essential part of the building: a moulded cornice terminates the wall at the top and throws rain-water clear of the wall surface, a central pillared porch gives dignity to the entrance and the tall first-floor windows have wrought-iron balconies of geometrical design.

These enrichments, applied with taste to a building, gave it grace, and the particular mode of application – for infinite variety was possible within the conventions – gave it personality. The fact that the style was universally accepted meant that the great architects, when they had opportunities of producing important and original work, could do so in a language everyone understood; and the ordinary architects and builders, however little imagination and originality they might have, could never go far wrong. That is why the minor architecture of this period, the cottages in rural villages and the squares and crescents in the towns, have so much appeal for us today. They not only have the mellow charm of most things that are old; they also have order and consistency – a sense of the part being related to the whole – that contrasts strongly with the confusion of our own surroundings. The dullest buildings all have the qualities of reasonableness and reticence that we only achieve at our best, while the finest buildings have an assurance and maturity that we have recently been too uncertain of ourselves ever to reach. This is my apology for referring rather often to the eighteenth century here and elsewhere in this book. Many other periods, of course, produced architecture of equal merit, but the eighteenth century is the most recent period when a single style prevailed, and as it is comparatively recent, sufficient buildings, and even whole streets and towns, of the period remain as proof of the virtue of consistency and uniformity. Apart from a number of individual and important buildings, such as the great medieval cathedrals, the fortresses, and country mansions, the architectural richness of England lies in the Georgian streets of her country towns, the squares in her cities, and the small houses for farmers and country squires that still abound throughout the countryside. Other European countries (though in a smaller degree, because most of them were less prosperous in the eighteenth century) have the same inheritance; so have the eastern states of the U.S.A. Such buildings are the anonymous products of a uniform architectural language such as we need today more than anything else. For the individual genius is a law to himself in any period; it is quality in the mass of building that makes an age of civilized architecture.

Now in the eighteenth century this quality of consistency was closely bound up with the social structure. The educated class was a small one numerically, but it was still the ruling class and took an active interest in architecture. There was therefore only one source of style, only one mould of fashion. The uniform pattern of architecture of which we have been speaking was handed down from the aristocratic patron and the private architect whom he took under his wing to every builder and small provincial architect, who educated themselves in the rules prescribed from above with the aid of the innumerable books filled with engravings of architectural types and details that were published for their guidance. They often interpreted the originals crudely, but as an honest rustic version of the more sophisticated original. Often their rougher methods simply produced a more vigorous, but equally sound, character. In any case, the rightness of taste remained; a rightness that came from complete mastery of the language they were using.

But this satisfactory state of affairs, simply because it was so bound up with the existing social order, could not last. Not only does the very rigidity of a system itself breed its own destruction: after a rational age the pendulum inevitably swings towards a romantic age: but worldly affairs change, and at the beginning of the nineteenth century the whole social structure was altered out of recognition in the space of a few years. At the same time scientific progress also changed the whole basis of architecture in the technical sense.

The first signs of the disintegration of the established architecture of the eighteenth century appeared when people began to take an interest in the research that scholars were doing into the architecture of past ages. At first it was only an academic interest, but eventually it was to change the whole attitude to architecture on the part of the very people from whom architecture drew its ideas. For it was fashionable, if you were an educated man, to take an interest in these investigations of the antique, and before long ideas picked up from antique periods began to creep into the houses of men of taste: Chinese wall-papers, Pompeiian decorations, Egyptian sculpture, and Greek ornament. There thus came into being the idea, which we have already remarked as characteristic of the subsequent Victorian age, of reviving past styles according to fancy; of style being merely the costume of the architect's choice.

Therefore, although it is not incorrect to say that the industrial revolution was the cause of the breakdown of the old order in architecture, as in everything else, the first signs of a change of viewpoint came earlier, in the deliberate revival of ancient styles. Although they were at the same time responsible for some of the most delightful things of their period, the culprits were people like the Adam brothers, who introduced Greek motifs into their designs, and Horace Walpole, who fostered the fashion for Gothic. The Greek Revival which was the most widespread of these first stylistic revivals, did not itself show much evidence of the important changes it foreshadowed. It lasted from about 1790 until the beginning of Queen Victoria's reign, but under its influence architects continued to maintain the Georgian respect for rules and good taste. Even the Gothic Revival of the same period, inspired by literary fashion and romantic leanings, was only a change of mannerism. One might say that it spoke in the same language with a different accent: the old social order was still intact. The principle of conformity was, however, loosened, and when momentous technical, industrial, and social changes undermined the position of architecture, it had no habits more deeply rooted than those of fashion to keep it related to real life.

When the industrial revolution did come it brought changes of incredible magnitude. First of all, steam-power replaced handwork, and factories were enabled to produce goods in quantities unheard of before; secondly, the spread of education among the masses brought to an end the domination of the aristocracy; thirdly, a new social class (the merchants and industrialists) became rich, and were either, on account of their newly-acquired wealth, automatically promoted to an equal position with the aristocracy, or else they formed the powerful new middle class, but in neither case had they the education or stability to become leaders of taste in the way the old ruling class had been; and, finally, an astonishing increase in the population transformed England – where the industrial revolution first took place – almost overnight from a primarily agricultural country into an urban industrial one.

Whole books could be written – and several have been – on the industrial revolution and all it meant; but what it meant to architecture is simple enough. It meant the end of an era. The eighteenth century's aristocratic system of culture was unable to accommodate itself to such drastic changes and that new interest in exotic styles which we have already observed developed into a romantic movement, offering architects an excuse to escape from problems that were becoming more and more different from the simple problems of taste that they had been accustomed to. The housing of the industrial masses, for example, could not be solved by means of connoisseurship and a taste for the picturesque; so before long – by the time the Gothic Revival had established itself – the real building work of the country was being done quite independently of the architectural profession.

The principal architectural use the new machinery was put to was the imitation by mechanical means of the ornament evolved by craftsmen in previous ages, and the imitation in cheap materials of the appearance of expensive ones. The new middle class delighted to surround itself with evidence of its recent rise in the world. Mechanical ornament was cheap, showy, and easy to produce. So we got that elaboration of ornament that is so characteristic of much Victorian work.

It was left to the engineers to use the new science creatively. With few exceptions any work of other than purely pictorial merit produced by architects after the industrial revolution had reached its height owed its existence to the survival, for one reason or another, of eighteenth-century conditions. Fine stucco terraces were created under royal or aristocratic patronage (though it will often be found that such terraces are only imposing façades with shameless slums behind), decent middle-class housing was put up by builders still adhering to some remnant of the Georgian code of rules, and the simple tradition of the Greek Revival was pursued here and there in a desultory academic way. But architects as a profession had largely become antiquarians and had entirely become individualists. Lacking a real social basis, architecture had become far too much a personal affair. This makes the architecture of the nineteenth century a fascinating subject to study, so complexly are the various personal, literary, and other influences interwoven, but it is evidence again that architects had lost touch with the real business of architecture. The idea of the celebrity-architect, that is, the idea that the design of a building must always reflect the personality of its architect as a painting does of its painter, is indeed one of the principal legacies of the nineteenth century that we still have with us. But architecture is only to a limited extent a personal art.

This age of period revivals, which regards architecture as rather an expensive kind of sculpture, designed – often brilliantly – out of bits belonging to past ages, but without consideration for the changed conditions under which it is produced, has lasted till the present day and is only now being displaced by the modern architecture that we are considering in this book.

It has been necessary to indicate the changes that architecture underwent rather over a hundred years ago in order to remind ourselves how it managed to become so completely detached from reality, and at the same time to observe what were the conditions under which it was once healthy and sane. But we have only half answered the question asked in the title of this chapter. We have seen why the modern movement in architecture began by being revolutionary: before it could create anything good of its own it had to correct the false position which architects had allowed society to push them into. But we have not yet seen why, when the architect's tasks are once more adjusted to reality, the resulting 'modern' architecture appears so strikingly different from anything that has gone before.

The truth is that although architects have today to go back, in a sense, and pick up the threads of a common architectural language at the point where they became unrecognizably entangled by the break-up of eighteenth-century society, they find it necessary to go back much further than that: back to first principles. The whole job of architecture has so changed in recent times, that it is necessary to think out many old problems afresh and to deal with other problems that architects never met before.

People who do not understand how the design of buildings comes about, criticize modern architecture by saying that, after all, architecture has always had the same function to fulfil, that of sheltering and accommodating the various kinds of human activity, so what is all this talk about a modern architecture for modern people, as though modern people were a new and different race who did not still get up in the morning and go to bed at night and go to school and play games in the way they have done for centuries? Thereby they suggest that modern architects are only being different in order to be perverse, but they forget that they are looking at people as individuals, whereas architecture also – in fact chiefly – has to cater for people as Society. And the needs of Society have changed out of all recognition in the last hundred years.

There is only one important respect in which the lives of people as a whole have not changed; that is in the unit on which the organization of their life is based, which is still the biological unit of the family. So the one-family house, at any rate when it is placed by itself, as in the country, is an architectural type which presents no fundamentally new problems. Those of us who happen to live in, say, the kind of eighteenth-century house that we described a little while back, do so without noticeable discomfort. It is not so old as to be too primitive in its lighting and sanitation (the latter has probably been modernized, in any case) and it is planned in a rational, straightforward way that allows us to fit into it very comfortably. So near our own requirements are such old houses in fact, that the best modern houses often bear a remarkable resemblance to them, without ever consciously imitating them. Modern houses do also, of course, differ from eighteenth-century houses, but not fundamentally; only in the ways in which the buildings of one century must inevitably differ from those of another, which is a different matter.

24

When we come to consider other architectural types, however, we find quite a different state of affairs. New problems have been produced by, for instance, the change-over from an agricultural to an industrial economy and by the development of rapid transport. If domestically we remain what we always have been, socially we are without doubt a new race.

The most important of the new needs that modern architecture has to provide for are connected with the growth of cities. There were cities in past centuries, but their population was seldom densely packed. They had more the character of our own market towns, however much more important they may have been in relation to the rest of the country. The large town or city as we know it is entirely a modern conception. It originated when the growing population crowded into new centres to serve the new industries, which resulted in such an increase in land-values in the middle of the cities, and such a density of population, that the traditional forms of housing were no longer practicable. So we got the blocks of flats and tenements that are so typical of town architecture. And at the same time we got suburbs, as soon as improved transport allowed people who had work to do in the city to live some distance outside it. The increase in the density of population has made the utilization of the available space much more of a problem. This, too, is bound up with transport, not only because the modern city must be most carefully planned with room for motor and other transport, but because the new suburbs have created fresh problems by cutting off the town from the open country that used to be just outside its doors. These are the problems of planning that have to be dealt with by the new profession that has come into being since they arose; the town-planning profession. But so far as individual types of building are concerned these new conditions have produced one important new type: the block of flats. Other entirely new types are railway stations and garages, power stations and industrial plants of many sorts. But equally important is the fact that buildings for purposes that are not themselves new, have to answer such changed needs that they are virtually new architectural types: schools have to accommodate a national education system on an entirely new scale, hospitals have to serve modern medical science, and the department-store has replaced the old-fashioned market.

Thus architects must go back to first principles in order to solve problems for which history has no precedents. By going back to first principles I mean something more than abandoning the slavery to revived styles. I mean avoiding a preconceived idea of what a building is going to look like (which is the basis of the Victorian view of architecture as large-scale sculpture), but, instead, working out its appearance simultaneously with its needs, taking absolutely nothing for granted. For the compromise of leaving off the period ornament but retaining the academic formulae by no means produces modern architecture. It may produce buildings that are superficially imposing, like Shell-Mex House or Broadcasting House in London, but they will possess neither the aesthetic appeal of a real modern building nor the pictorial charms of the honest period piece. The omission of period ornament brings solid-looking masonry exteriors no nearer to being true to the steel skeletons that are almost certainly concealed behind them.

By looking at the task of designing a building first as a practical problem that must be solved in a practical way; a problem of accommodating so many people so that they can pursue certain activities comfortably, conveniently, and economically, and at the same time with the feeling of pleasure in their surroundings, a new view of architecture can be obtained that puts all the mumbo-jumbo of academic style into its proper perspective. It may be necessary to emphasize that in modern architecture practical considerations are not everything, with beauty compelled to take its chance. On the contrary, the production of beauty is part of the process of design, not an afterthought in the way of applied decoration, and its liveliness and appropriateness is thereby increased. This simple way of looking at architecture may appear very obvious, but if it had been kept more clearly in people's minds during the past hundred years, our cities would be less hideous places today.

Modern architects, faced with new problems, must go back to elementary principles. But one difficulty is that even though we may be aware of the new needs and be willing to seek a new kind of building that will satisfy them, we are not always aware of their exact nature. The present age is still a transitional one. It is not only a question of new types of building being needed, but of the needs themselves being in many cases insufficiently defined for the appropriate architectural type to be clearly apparent. That is why modern architecture is still experimental: architects are experimenting in the needs of building – in what architecture can do for society – as well as in technique. In a more settled period like the eighteenth century, the types of building were fixed because building needs were fixed. The architect's programme was a definite and a familiar one, and he was able to concentrate his energies on the task of perfecting his few types of building and inventing new variations of them. But today, when conditions are so rapidly changing and problems are mostly without precedent, his task is far more complicated. If, for example, he has to design a school, he has first to analyse its needs right from the beginning; he has almost to plan educational methods, if not by himself at least in collaboration with the educationist. In preparing a housing scheme he has to study matters like movements of population and the relation between income and rent. In planning a factory he has to know all about the product that is to be made. Often the finished building is itself only a stage in his experiments, by which he learns to do better next time. For reasons like these the most successful modern buildings have generally belonged to types for which the programme is quite definite: buildings housing a clear routine, such as factories and hospitals. But as time passes and their collective experience increases, the modern architects get nearer to providing the world with that accepted architectural language, in which the results of endless experiments are incorporated, which is the sign of a mature architecture. It is doubtful, however, whether in our complex civilization we shall ever be able to reduce building types and elements – the words, as it were, that form our architectural language – to the small number that the eighteenth and previous centuries were able to manage with, however successful we are in sorting our experiments out into the basis of a modern style. That is why absolute open-mindedness is an essential part of the modern architects' method, and will continue to be so after the present experimental phase is over.

So, to sum up, the principal reason why a new architecture is coming into existence is that the *needs* of this age are in nearly every case totally different from the needs of previous ages, and so cannot be satisfied by methods of building that belong to any age but the present. We *can* satisfy them in the practical sense, by utilizing modern building technique and modern scientific inventions to the full; and we can satisfy them in the aesthetic sense, both by being honest craftsmen in our own materials and by taking special advantage of the opportunities these materials offer of creating effects and qualities in tune with our own times. For example, instead of grafting antique ornaments on to new structures, as is often done today, thereby making them inconvenient and expensive as well as ridiculous, or else constraining the new structures within limits imposed by old ones – clothing a modern steel frame in a mass of masonry, to get that effect of solidity that was quite rightly admired in Classical buildings of solid stone construction, but is entirely false today; instead of either of these timid expedients we can make the most of the precision and machine finish that is so characteristic of modern technique and set out to explore, as our predecessors the Gothic architects so bravely did, the aesthetic possibilities of lightness and poise.

The more strictly practical effect of modern science on the design of buildings is discussed in the next two chapters.

CHAPTER III

ARCHITECTURE AND MACHINERY

THROUGHOUT history both the general appearance of buildings and their style of ornament have been determined by the knowledge of building technique available, as well as by the materials used and the tools with which they were worked and, of course, as well by fashion and taste. Roman architecture, for example, developed so far from the Greek model on which it was based because the Romans discovered the use of the round arch and the vault, whereas the Greeks built only with columns and beams; and Gothic church architecture blossomed out of the simple solidity of the Norman period into more and more daring feats of construction, chiefly as the medieval architect-engineers learnt the science of mechanics and discovered thereby exactly how small a pier could safely carry the load of a roof, and how it was possible to transfer some of the downward thrust on to a series of flying buttresses; but, more fundamentally, it originated in the pointed arch, which was itself a product of experiments in vaulted roofing with the small size stones produced by contemporary quarrying methods and the absence of slave labour.

Modern architecture is conditioned by the same sort of factors. We know more exactly than our ancestors how materials behave in different circumstances, and we have invented or discovered a number of new materials. For both these reasons our range or vocabulary is greater, and for the former reason we have no excuse for building unscientifically. We cannot avoid the obligation to build scientifically. In no past age did men build less skilfully than they knew how.

But neither the introduction of these new materials, such as structural steel and reinforced concrete, nor the advent of all the mechanical aids to comfortable living, such as air-conditioning and refrigeration, which we are so rich in today – both results of our modern industrial economy – themselves produce a revolution in architecture. They only represent the natural development of traditional architecture. For the architect has always made it part of his job to adapt his methods to suit new materials and mechanical contrivances. And he has successfully assimilated into his practice in the past many innovations more startling than those of the present. The difference between the heating system of the Elizabethan manor with its grouped chimney flues and that of the modern house with its central heating and electrical wiring – or even the modern hospital containing every kind of built-in equipment – is only a difference of degree. The architect may have more complications of this kind to think about – the telephone and radio as well as fresh air and smoke – in the same way that he has more materials at his disposal, but the way he goes about his task of incorporating them all in a building without intruding their presence or interfering with their efficiency remains the same.

One thing, however, which has made modern architecture different in *kind* from the architecture of the past is also connected with modern industry, particularly with its dependence on power production: namely, the factory system. The actual labour of producing the parts of a building is now centred in the factories instead of being left in the hands of the individual workman. At one time the workmen arrived on the site of a proposed building with all their raw materials and the tools to shape them with; stone or timber for the walls, more timber for floors, doors, and windows, lime for plastering the walls; and they constructed the building on the spot, manufacturing as they went along whatever was needed in the way of doors and windows, sometimes even quarrying stone, clay, or sand on the site. Later, for convenience, the doors and window-frames were made in the builder's joinery-shops, and hinges, bolts, and other ironwork made at the local blacksmiths, but even then they were made as needed specially for the occasion. The first important example of what we now call 'prefabrication' – that is, the manufacture of ready-made building parts – was the brick industry. The earliest bricks may have been moulded from clay dug upon the site, but as soon as bricks were in common use (in England by the end of the fifteenth century) brickfields were started to fulfil a permanent demand, and these were the first building-material factories. Since then, factories having become the normal way of making things, the process has been tremendously accelerated. Today a large proportion of building jobs is done in a factory: the windows – probably metal windows – arrive ready made, so do steel beams and columns, so do doors and sinks, baths and all equipment. The erection of a building is being changed into a process of assembling ready-made parts, and is going farther in this direction every day. The completely prefabricated home, delivered to the site in a lorry in the form of factory-made sections that can be put together ready for occupation in a few days, has already been tried out.

In the case of larger buildings, the carcass – usually a steel frame – arrives in the form of finished units ready to be riveted together, and the only jobs done with raw materials on the spot are plastering and painting. Concreting, of course, for the foundations has to be done on the spot; that is, the concrete has to be poured into the foundation trenches while it is still wet; but even here the practice is growing of having it delivered ready mixed – in those revolving drums mounted on lorries – thereby doing all that can be done in advance; and ready-made units of concrete walling have been invented, which may be regarded as the up-to-date equivalent of bricks. The former are large and therefore quick and easy to handle with modern tackle, while the latter were devised in the size and shape most suited to the bricklayer's hand.

The practical advantages of prefabrication are twofold: it is quicker and it does away with uncertainty. Speed in building is important in these days because of the high cost of land: the time during which such an expensive commodity is out of use must be reduced to a minimum. And partly or wholly prefabricated methods of construction save time on the job not only because everything is ready in the factory beforehand but because prefabrication means a change-over from wet to dry construction. Anyone who has had to wait for a new house to be ready before he could move in knows how much time is spent waiting for concrete to set or plaster to dry out before the next operation can be proceeded with. Prefabrication does away with uncertainty because it means that the whole building is made of standard parts whose behaviour is known and has been tested. Any defective part can be replaced, and there is no uncertainty whether this or that feature of the building will work satisfactorily.

That is how factory production affects building technique. But how does the new building technique – especially prefabrication – affect the appearance of buildings? First, of course, directly through the new factory-made materials themselves and the things they can do: span great distances, carry heavy loads, or merely shine in the sun instead of melting into the background. We will come to that later. But secondly – and equally important – through the effect on design of the specialization of labour. In fact this is one clue to the fundamental difference, which I have already mentioned, between modern architecture and the architecture of previous centuries: one reason why architecture can never be the same again.

The difference is this: that before this highly industrialized age, the workman who worked on a building was responsible directly for one part of the building, which he could see growing before his eyes. He may only have shaped the rafters for the roof, or he may have carved the ornament round a Gothic door or moulded the plaster ceiling of a Georgian country house; but the building was a direct result of his efforts, and the quality of its design – in many cases its actual nature – depended on his skill. Nowadays, on the other hand, his counterpart is the man who minds a machine in a factory; who is not concerned with the use to which the particular object he is making will be put or the effect it will have on a finished building. The building in which it is to be used has, in fact, probably not yet been thought of. The manufacturer is producing a quantity of whatever it is he makes – metal windows or steel beams or door-handles – for an estimated future demand.

It is true that there are workmen employed on the building itself, even in these days of prefabrication; but, as I have already pointed out, they tend more and more to become simply the assemblers of ready-made parts, like the men who work on the assembly-line in an up-to-date motor-car plant. The latter are highly skilled workmen, but they cannot said to be making motor-cars themselves. This is being done collectively by the men at the machines which separately turn out the hundreds of different parts.

Now the whole tradition of craftsmanship on which the architectural style of previous centuries was based consisted of first the fashioning and then the embellishment of parts of a building by a set of craftsmen who between them imagined and made the whole building. Even when, as during the Renaissance period, there was a controlling mind in the person of the architect, the individual craftsmen knew the building they were working on and their contribution was automatically related to the whole. Always in the past ornament was created as part of the process of making something, wherein an individual gave something of himself in the process. But ornament divorced from handicraft is not the same thing, and nowadays the man who makes things has no longer any say in their design. Much of the value of handicraft ornament, moreover, lay in its virtuosity. It represented an effort of workmanship. It stood for someone's skill and patience. But now that machines can turn out any quantity of ornament with ease there is less virtue in it. At best it is only a sign of wealth – to be able to afford a more complicated machine – which has little to do with architecture.

That is why Victorian machine ornament, when it mechanically imitated hand-carving, produced bad architecture; and that is also why modern architecture tends to do without ornament in the sense of carving or applied decoration. It is not because we are puritans nowadays, or because we have not succeeded in thinking out a 'modern' style of ornament, or because modern life is too much of a rush, or for any of the nonsensical reasons that are customarily given. Modern buildings are not enriched with conventional ornament because their parts are made by machines, and applied ornament is not the machine's method of beautification.

Complication and richness have their place in modern architecture; but complication by itself is no longer a virtue. It is sometimes mistaken for one, notably by the people who make cheap furniture. If you want simple, well-made furniture, you have to pay highly for it, as for a luxury, because nearly all mass-produced furniture is covered with nasty machine-made ornament, presumably because either the manufacturer or the trade buyer or the public thinks it an improvement. Though possibly the ornament is stuck on to cover up the cracks.

This misuse of machinery was what William Morris had in

mind when he campaigned against mid-Victorian ugliness and insincerity and tried to revive a genuine spirit of crafts-manship. He understood that the vitality had gone from everyday design because the men who designed things no longer made them, and vice versa; but he wanted to abolish machines, as being chiefly responsible, which was trying to do the impossible. He and his followers would have done more good by admitting that machinery is only an instrument, to be used well or badly, and campaigning for a more intelligent use of it. William Morris saw man as a creative animal being overwhelmed by the machinery he had produced, in the same way that, as a political philosopher, he saw man the individual being submerged in the system of competitive capitalism which he had produced. To his far-seeing mind ideas about art were inseparable from ideas about Society. Today the machinery he loathed has increased in power and complexity, and art (including architecture) is still suffering from confusion of purpose and ideas, owing to our failure to adapt ourselves to the possession of machinery, and make it provide for us some modern substitute for the direct craft tradition of the medieval period or the code of discipline and taste that the autocracy of the seventeenth and eighteenth centuries provided. Society and art are still indivisible, so it is probable that the reform most needed to put art right with itself is a social reform: some change that would enable the creative designer and the machines he uses to be directly available once more to Society as a whole, instead of serving the whims of fashion, money, or snobbery. It has been said before that great architecture is more a product of the times than of personalities.

However, such questions are outside the scope of this book. What we are concerned with is not the social results of machinery as reflected in architecture, but the direct effect of machinery on the appearance of architecture itself. And this we can study. For, in spite of our general failure during the past hundred years to adapt ourselves to the new conditions that industrialization has brought, we have in modern architecture a phenomenon of modern life that is remarkable for having done so. Modern architecture is truly of this age in that it does recognize that machinery and factories are the essence of the age. It exploits them aesthetically as well as practically, finding new beauties inherent in the products of machinery instead of merely regretting, like Morris and other nineteenth-century reformers, that old beauties have passed away.

It is a little misleading, however, to define modern architecture as the architecture of the machine age; not because it is untrue but because it suggests that it is thereby of a limited and inhuman kind. There is an idea called 'functionalism' that is often associated with modern architecture; in fact even by well-informed people modern architecture is often described as 'functionalist'. As this description is entirely untrue it may be as well, before we continue our examination of the actual effect of machine production on architectural design, to give some attention to laying this particular bogey.

It is difficult to say when the idea of functionalism was first put about. It is present, with reservations, in many writings about architecture from the Roman Vitruvius onwards; but in these cases, of course, the reservations are all-important. For architecture, being a practical art, must always depend to some degree on function, a fact which all sensible writers on the subject have recognized. But the idea of absolute functionalism – which can be defined as the idea that good architecture is produced automatically by strict attention to utility, economy, and other purely practical considerations – is a more recent phenomenon. It is doubtful, as a matter of fact, whether this theory in its absolute form has ever been seriously held by practising architects; they would soon have found that it prevented them from exercising their functions at all: but as there is nevertheless a popular belief that the modern kind of architecture is functionalist it is necessary to discuss the theory at some length, if only as a way of showing what a modern architecture is by explaining one important thing that it is not.

The confusion arose largely through the theorizing and propaganda about modern architecture that was current during the first quarter of this century. A new architecture was then emerging from the confusion of the nineteenth century, and the most striking difference between the new architecture and the old was that the former laid stress on the utilitarian basis of architecture which the latter had largely ignored. Modern architects took the opportunity provided by all the new materials and methods that science had made available to rescue architecture from the stagnation of stylistic revivals. They found it necessary, as I have already described, to return to first principles, and among the first principles of architecture is that it should do the job it has to do as efficiently as possible. It is not surprising, therefore, that when architects and writers tried to explain to the world what the new architecture was all about, they should have stressed this practical side of it as its special virtue. In some instances, moreover, as in the writings of the famous French architect and propagandist Le Corbusier, an extreme functionalist attitude was deliberately taken up as the best way of instilling into the public the importance of being practical first and foremost. His famous pronouncement, '*une maison est une machine à habiter*', served very well as a slogan advertising the simple, but at that time revolutionary, conception of architecture as primarily a matter of shelter. His technique of deliberate over-simplification did succeed in doing a lot to clear away the sentimentalities and prejudices that had come to form so large a proportion of people's views on architecture. That Le Corbusier himself, as an architect, never thought of buildings as being nothing but machines is very clear from the buildings themselves. He is one of the most imaginative architects of modern times, and his buildings are remarkable for their freedom from rule-of-thumb designing. He never does anything just because it has been done before or because it is customary, and he therefore fulfils absolutely his ideal of rational design; but at the same time his buildings are full of poetic quality that is pure art and very far from being the product of mechanical thinking.

Le Corbusier also, in his very influential writings* about architecture, was one of the first people to draw attention to the beauty of machines themselves; to illustrate an aeroplane, a motor-car, and a turbine in a book about architectural design; and this, too, has led people to suppose that modern architects believe that beautiful building can arise automatically from mechanical efficiency.

The difference between these two things, beautiful building and mechanical efficiency, is, of course, the difference between architecture and engineering. It is true that modern architects are influenced by the work of modern engineers. It is natural that this should be so. For all the new shapes and materials that made the unexplored possibilities of modern architecture so exciting, arrived in the beginning by way of engineering: steel was used with thrilling results for bridges before it was used in architecture, and many architects first saw the beauty of machine products in the mechanical equipment – the power installations, the kitchen equipment, even the electric lamps – that science provided and demanded that they fit into their buildings, even while the latter were still enslaved to the ritual of historical styles. The great en-

*Particularly *Vers une Architecture*, published in 1922 and translated into English in 1927 under the title *Towards a New Architecture* – see bibliography.

gineering works that modern science and industry produced had a breath-taking beauty, and it was easy for the architect, confused by contradictory aesthetic creeds, to feel that he would ask nothing better than to have designed a building as directly appealing and as moving as this electric pylon or that enormous floating dock, which were primarily utilitarian; and therefore perhaps architecture would do best to follow the same method. But architecture, as modern architects fully appreciate, goes deeper than engineering. The beauty of the new structures that engineering has introduced into the landscape is genuine enough, and one's emotional reaction to them is natural, but this appeal is not really an architectural one. It is the appeal of size, simplicity, cleanness, and honesty; in fact of all the qualities that nineteenth-century academic architecture lacked. It is the appeal of a new world, inevitably stimulating to people who are becoming conscious that they live surrounded by the leavings of an old one, but it is not the *art* of a new world. One can admire things that possess some of the qualities that modern architecture should have, without taking them for modern architecture itself. One can also learn from them; and the important thing that modern architecture has learnt from engineering and machine design – from docks, power pylons, and aeroplanes – is first the technique of using new materials, secondly simplicity of line and honesty of expression, and thirdly the overwhelming grandeur of the fundamental architectural qualities, rhythm, scale, and contrast, which engineering uses anonymously and as if by chance. These qualities could instructively be compared with the pettiness of personal mannerism and individual expression that architecture was still wasting so much of its time on.

Even after we have said that it is engineering which is functional and architecture which is something more, it is often difficult to decide where one begins and the other ends. The 'something more' means that architectural design includes decisions or preferences made for non-utilitarian reasons, but we find that in all but the very simplest engineering problems, too, room is left for taste or preference to enter: choosing between certain alternatives or consciously varying the result within certain limits. Even engineering itself, that is to say, is seldom truly functional. The explanation of this difficulty is of course that the distinction between engineering and architecture is entirely an artificial one. It is only a hundred years old, having come about when the academic architects became primarily engrossed in styles early in the nineteenth century, when they came to regard the language of architecture as an end in itself instead of as the means to an end. We now recognize the works of the great engineers of this period – the bridges, harbours, railway-works, and the like of such men as Telford, I. K. Brunel, Robert Stephenson, and Joseph Paxton – which were designed with real creative imagination, as being among the best architecture of the early nineteenth century.

The harm that resulted from the splitting of the architect's functions is obvious. It put the architect in the position of being only the decorator of buildings designed by engineers, as though art was something that could be applied after the utilitarian side of the buildings was finished. Today it is part of the creed of the modern architect that the processes of constructing and designing a building are inseparable.

Modern architecture then, although it is dependent on machinery in many ways, remains *as an art* fundamentally a matter of the architect's discernment and imagination. He is free to use his imagination within the limits of utility. But if utility and art are properly coordinated one does not impose limits on the other. On the contrary, the utilitarian aspect of architecture provides a basis on which the architect's artistic sense can build something of more than utilitarian value. This of course is true of all good architecture; the difference being that nowadays the architect's material is largely machine-produced and machine-finished, which strongly influences his aesthetic ideals.

From machines themselves he has learnt the charm of simplicity and precision. He has learnt the value of eliminating everything unnecessary, not so much for reasons of economy as because the process of elimination brings out the essential character of structure. Much of the beauty of an electricity pylon, as of a Gothic spire, lies in its spare economy of means, indicating its designer's complete mastery over the material of which it is constructed. Secondly, machines, as we have seen, have lessened the virtue in elaborate ornament because they have abolished the point of doing something because it is difficult. This does not mean that richness has gone from architecture. Machine-produced shapes and textures lend themselves to infinite complication. The modern equivalent of applied ornament, however, largely lies in the natural qualities of materials themselves; in the grain and surface of beautiful woods, in the sheen of new metal alloys, and in the contrasting texture of fabrics; all used with the exactness of finish that machines have introduced into architecture. Indeed, the eventual result of the precision with which machinery works may be an increase in our own awareness of the subtleties produced by precision. Our perceptions in the past have been blunted by the vulgarities of architectural clichés, by the meaningless masses of material hung on to architecture; but the new architecture gives us a chance to develop a more subtle appreciation of proportion and rhythm such as set the standards of eighteenth-century taste. One can foresee a new connoisseurship coming into play, developing out of our acceptance of modern architecture's mechanistic basis.

One other thing which tends to reduce the high standards

we might otherwise have, apart from the quantity of *vague* architecture we see every day around us, is the fact that so many of us live in surroundings that are only adapted, not designed, for their purpose: largely old-fashioned houses converted into flats, for example, and houses not originally wired for electricity, so that the cables run all over the walls instead of being neatly concealed. We get accustomed to accepting as a matter of habit, in converted buildings, shifts and approximations that the ideals of modern architecture would never tolerate. And the standards we demand follow suit, for you cannot train your perceptions to judge things according to two standards of finish simultaneously.

Any discussion of the influence machinery has had on architecture must not omit the important part played by standardization. I have already discussed the growth of mass production of building parts in factories, beginning with the first brickfields and only ending with the completely pre-fabricated building. But the fact of standardization – which results from mass-production – has a strong influence on design as well as on technique. It puts great responsibility on the industrial designer: the man who invents the object which the machine merely copies an infinite number of times. Complete prefabrication, of course, would simply bring the architect into the factory as designer; but this degree of pre-fabrication could only apply to types of buildings in which the needs are more or less standardized. In more complex buildings their varying needs and the problems of planning in relation to other buildings will always demand a specially thought-out solution. So the architect's job is not becoming a less responsible one, but under present-day conditions he is also dependent on the industrial designer for the quality of the standard parts he uses so much. The latter must take some of the responsibility of making the most of the archi-tectural opportunities offered by modern building technique;

for a good type of metal window, sensible and good-looking wash-basins, well-designed door-handles, and many more such details – besides furniture and fabrics – all play a big part in the final quality of the whole. And the production of such things as these in factories, according to standard patterns, should bring about a high quality of design, because it enables the collective experience of designers to be pooled. Instead of each individual craftsman having to start from the beginning, making his own experiments and mistakes, each new design can build on the experience of previous ones. It is by this process of gradual improvement that the design of aeroplanes and motor-cars is perfected, and this is what architecture can adopt from their example.

CHAPTER IV

NEW MATERIALS AND METHODS

MUCH of the unexpectedness of modern architecture is due to the new materials that have become available during the last half century. The inventions of science can be used either to do the old things more conveniently or cheaply, or to do things that could not be done before. Architects have used modern building technique in both of these ways. You would not think, to look at it, that the Ritz Hotel, Piccadilly, built in 1906, is of historic importance as being the first steel-framed building put up in London; but, on the other hand, it is quite evident that the Peter Jones store in Sloane Square (see Plate 29) is of skeleton frame construction. Its whole design is based on the advantages a steel frame offers: that of being able, for example, to keep the framework, which supports the floor, some distance inside the face of the building, making the outside walls only a screen, taking no weight but their own, so that on the ground floor continuous show-windows can be provided, uninterrupted by columns. Compare this again with a store like Selfridge's in Oxford Street, where the steel frame is encased in the trappings of a Renaissance palace, which include massive stone piers on the ground floor, cutting into the shop window space. The whole appearance of Peter Jones's, moreover, is obviously inspired by its skeleton construction. There can be no disputing which, Peter Jones's or the Ritz or Selfridge's, is the most sensible and lively modern building.

The most important of the new materials are structural steel and reinforced concrete. It is necessary to stress the adjectives 'structural' and 'reinforced', because steel as a material was of course known for centuries before it was applied to building, and concrete, in the form of masses of solid walling made by mixing stones and cement, was used widely by the Romans. But steel beams and columns are a product of modern industry and only date from the middle of the last century. The immediate predecessor of steel was cast iron, which came in with the growth of the big iron foundries early in the nineteenth century, and was the chief material used by the great engineers of that period, whose work I have already mentioned. The Crystal Palace, first erected in Hyde Park for the 1851 Exhibition, was constructed in cast iron. Soon afterwards, in 1855, Bessemer invented his 'converter process' which made possible the mass-production of steel, and as the advantages of steel beams and stanchions became apparent they gradually superseded cast iron. The advantages of the former over the latter are that steel ('mild' steel is the variety used in building) is more resilient and therefore stronger under all kinds of loading and in all circumstances. Cast iron is only equally strong when directly loaded, being too brittle to stand other kinds of strain. It is also less reliable, as the strength of different pieces varies considerably.

The form in which steel is most commonly used, both as beams or stanchions, is that of an I, consisting of thick flanges (to which flat plates are sometimes bolted to give extra thickness) kept apart by a thinner strip or 'web'. This shape, which is produced in rolling mills, by passing the steel through shaped rollers, resists the various stresses set up in a beam while using the minimum of material. The elimination of unnecessary material in a steel beam is much more important than in, say, a wooden one, not only in order that material shall not be wasted but because the steel itself is so heavy that too much of its strength would otherwise be expended in supporting its own weight, in addition to that of the floor or roof it is intended to carry.

Reinforced concrete was invented in France, by the engineers Hennebique and Coignet, in the nineties of last century, though in 1867 another Frenchman, Monier, had patented some flower-pots in which the same principle was used, and in 1885 an Englishman, William Simmons, put up a building in Lincoln's Inn Fields in which a primitive use of the same principle occurred in the construction. As its name implies, it is a composite material. The point of it is this: concrete by itself, which is really a kind of stone manufactured by mixing wet cement and sand with pebbles or coarse gravel and allowing it to set, is very strong, just as stone is, from the point of view of the direct weight it will stand – what engineers call its crushing strength – but it is relatively weak in other ways. It will soon fracture under any kind of stress other than direct weight. Now a beam spanning between two points – the commonest structural form – is simultaneously stressed in two ways. The upper half of it is in compression; that is, the tendency is for its particles to be crushed together; while the lower half is in tension; that is, the tendency is for the particles to be pulled apart. That this is so can easily be understood by taking a piece of wood sufficiently slender to be flexible and bending it as though it were a loaded beam. From the way it bends it is clear that the top surface is being compressed and the bottom surface stretched, and if it were bent to breaking point the fibres of the top surface would be found to have been bruised and crushed and those of the lower surface to have been torn apart. In a plain *concrete* beam of any considerable length, the upper half would stand any amount of compression, since the crushing strength of concrete is so great, but the lower half would soon break apart, since its tensile strength is weak. To span any but a short distance the beam would have to be impossibly massive, so much so that its own weight would be as much as it could carry. What is needed is some way of increasing the tensile strength of the lower part of the beam to equal the natural compressive strength in the upper part. This is done by embedding steel rods in appropriate positions in the lower half, steel being a material that is equally strong in compression and in tension. The steel rods are placed in position in the wooden moulds or 'forms' into which the concrete is poured when wet.

Reinforced concrete therefore is a material combining the crushing strength (and the ease with which it can be cast in any desired shape) of concrete with the tensile strength of steel, and all reinforced concrete structures are only an elaboration of this principle, though some are exceedingly complex. The steel rods have to be put exactly where the tensile stresses will come. For example, in the portion of a beam over its points of support the positions of the stresses are reversed. Imagine the piece of wood described above passing over an intermediate support and loaded either side of it. It will be understood that the tendency at this point is for it to bend in the reverse direction; the tension is along the top and the compression at the bottom, and the steel reinforcing rods have to slope upwards as these stresses change until immediately above the support they are running along the top surface instead of the bottom. Even this is comparatively straightforward, but arched roofs, for example, unevenly loaded columns, and spiral staircases present exceedingly complicated mathematical problems. And in recent years new developments, like 'pre-stressed' and 'shell' concrete, have allowed even greater strength to be obtained with an even more economical use of material.

The most obvious advantage of steel and reinforced concrete is that they will span very great distances. This first of all enables large spaces to be covered in easily and economically. The most important experiments that were made in the early days of steel construction were the huge exhibition halls, designed by the French engineers, De Dion, Gustave Eiffel, and Cottancin (Plate 6) for the Paris Exhibitions of 1878 and 1889; and later came such striking structures in reinforced concrete as the airship hangars at Orly, France (see Plate 10), put up in 1916 by Eugène Freyssinet.

Concrete and steel also allow architects to make openings in their walls of whatever size they want. Previously the size of the windows in a building was determined by the width of opening possible; that is, by the distance that could be spanned by a stone or wooden lintel or a brick arch. The whole exterior appearance of traditional buildings is based on this distance, for the appearance, particularly of classical buildings, is largely given by the spacing and proportion of the windows. It is not surprising, therefore, that the use of steel and concrete for construction (or the use of these materials to span wide openings in walls of brick or stone construction) should alone produce a revolution in architectural design. Furthermore, as a direct result of wider window openings, windows themselves have improved. Today we have numerous kinds of folding and sliding windows to fit into these wide openings, notably the kind that both slides and folds up like a concertina so that the whole of the window, possibly running the length of the room, can be thrown open to the air. When required (since plate glass in large sizes is another new material) whole walls can be built of glass, though in private houses, privacy and cosiness being important requirements, very large windows are not always wanted. But in offices, shops, and factories they are invaluable, and in sanatoriums and schools they have led to a tremendous improvement in health and efficiency. Even in private houses, if we want large areas of glass in some of the rooms, as we often do, being of a generation that boasts of being fond of light and air, we can have them without discomfort, since improved heating methods make it unnecessary even for rooms that are mostly window to be bleak and cold.

The use of steel and reinforced concrete has brought about another even more radical change in our conception of architecture. The normal way of using either of these materials is as a framework or skeleton. This means that weight-bearing walls disappear. The weight of floors and roofs is taken by the structural skeleton and the walls become screens whose purpose is to enclose the space within, to keep out the weather and to keep out sound. They can be made of glass, as pointed out above, wherever and to whatever size windows are needed, and they can be pushed out into bays or recessed to form alcoves; the whole building, indeed, as its weight is transferred to the ground only at a few small points, can be raised on these as on legs, so that the garden or street passes right underneath it (see Plate 17 and Plate 18, bottom). In fact the disappearance of the solid weight-bearing wall has introduced a new flexibility into planning, as walls and partitions can be placed quite independently of the few points of support. This, in its turn, has enabled architects to relate the planning of a building much more closely to its site. One might say that the hard and fast line between house and garden has been broken down; one is allowed to flow into the other through sliding walls that extend a room on to a garden ter-

---

REINFORCED CONCRETE. The diagrams on the facing page show the principle on which reinforced concrete (or 'ferro-concrete') construction is based. 1. A beam, showing the direction of the stresses that are set up in it. 2. A heavy load is too much for a plain concrete beam, owing to this material's low tensile strength. 3. In a reinforced concrete beam, the tensile stress is taken by steel rods inserted where the stress occurs, and the beam will now support very heavy loads. 4. When the beam passes over intermediate supports the stresses change their positions. 5. The steel reinforcement rods have to follow the stresses.

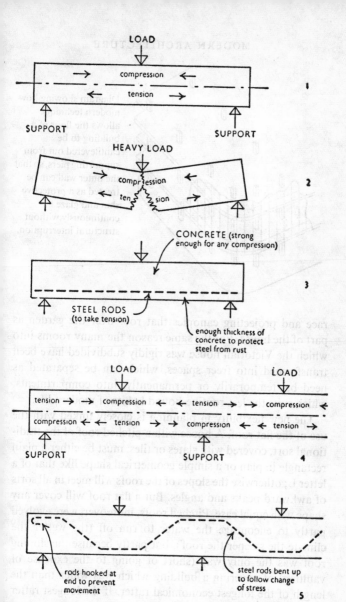

1

LOAD

compression → ←

tension ← →

SUPPORT   SUPPORT

2

HEAVY LOAD

compression ←

tension →

3

CONCRETE (strong
enough for any compression)

STEEL RODS
(to take tension)

enough thickness of
concrete to protect
steel from rust

4

LOAD   LOAD

tension → → compression ← ← tension → → compression ←

compression ← ← tension → → compression ← ← tension →

SUPPORT   SUPPORT

5

rods hooked at
end to prevent
movement

steel rods bent up
to follow change
of stress

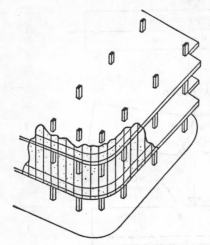

Diagram showing how modern technique allows the floor of a building to be cantilevered out from supporting piers, so that the outer wall can be treated as a protective skin and glazed continuously without structural interruption.

race and projecting canopies that roof over the garden as part of the house. For the same reason the many rooms into which the Victorian house was rigidly subdivided have been transformed into freer spaces, which can be separated as need be, temporarily or permanently, into compartments, which suits the less routine-bound habits of modern life.

The new flexibility in planning is closely linked with the use of the flat roof. A house with a pitched roof of the traditional sort, covered with slates or tiles, must be either a plain rectangle in plan or a simple geometrical shape like that of a letter L; otherwise the slopes of the roofs will meet in all sorts of awkward peaks and angles. But a flat roof will cover any shape with equal ease. Pitched roofs, moreover, were evolved partly to encourage the water to run off (the wetter the climate the steeper the roof), but partly because the sloping roof was the only way (short of going to the expense of vaulting) of covering a building which was wider than the length of the longest economical rafter. If the longest rafter was, say 20 feet, two sloping rafters of this length meeting at an angle would roof a building perhaps 30 feet wide. But now that wooden rafters of limited length can be replaced by steel beams and concrete slabs, and now that roof-covering materials such as asphalt and other bituminous products have been so improved that there is no question of flat roofs having practical disadvantages, they are naturally preferred by architects who appreciate being able to plan as freely as they wish.

Flat roofs of course need more careful insulation against the heat, but this, too, is not difficult with modern materials. One disadvantage they sometimes have in practice, however, is that they leave no room within the roof for putting all the water tanks and cisterns that a modern building needs, and these are apt to make an untidy jumble on the skyline, a failing particularly noticeable in these days of air travel, as a pitched-roofed building looks much neater and more shapely from the air than many flat-roofed ones. However, this is not a criticism of flat roofs, only of the way some architects use them. All that is needed is the forethought in planning that will allow these excrescences to be tucked away out of sight or disposed where they form part of the deliberate outline of the building.

While we are on the subject of flat roofs it is, perhaps, important to point out, just because they have for some reason become identified with controversies about modern architecture, that they are not in any sense inseparable from modern design. It is true that the modern architect very often chooses to use a flat roof, partly for the practical reasons given above, but equally because he likes them. He still tends to avoid emphasizing the pitched roof, perhaps because he is unconsciously aware that at the moment a modern architectural language has to compete with the survivals of other languages. Although the time is past when modern architecture had to exhibit its modernity, and roofs can be flat or sloping according to need, a flat roof has got a character in tune with this highly mechanized scientific age. It has a straightforwardness and repose and logic that is quite different from, say, the picturesque casualness of pointed gables and chimney stacks. In designing consistently with large plate-glass windows and flat roofs the architect is only making another step, partly practical and partly aesthetic, of the kind that was made when Tudor diamond-paned windows gave way to the large panes of glass of Georgian houses or when angular Elizabethan gables gave way to horizontal William-and-Mary cornices.

Frame construction has had another far-reaching effect on architectural design. The disappearance of the solid weight-bearing wall means that the massiveness of the wall has disappeared too. Masonry buildings of the Classical and Renaissance periods emphasized the solid construction of their walls, through which windows were pierced as holes. Modern buildings emphasize the lightness of their frame construction, in which the windows and the walls are only ways of filling in the space between the framework. Exploiting this difference, lightness and poise instead of solidity have become the architect's aim. The building appears poised on the ground instead of rooted into it, this characteristic being compatible with the elegance and precision that we have already discussed as something architects have learnt from machinery.

The skeleton nature of modern buildings has also produced several typical modern forms, which like the flat roof are used for a combination of practical and aesthetic reasons. Examples are the grid wall-pattern, giving expression to the difference between the structural framework and the filling (as at Peter Jones), and the strip window produced by canti-lever construction (that is, by projecting a roof out from its support: in one direction, like a gallows, or in several like a mushroom). Although the skeleton (or frame) is the typical form of reinforced concrete construction, it is not the only one, because another special characteristic of the material is the continuity that can be achieved between beams and walls and floor-slabs by pouring them as one piece, and from this arises the use of concrete as a thin membrane, which is bringing back into modern architecture several ancient forms like vaults and domes.

Another way of looking at the lightness and poise so characteristic of modern architecture is this: steel and concrete, as modern scientific materials, lend themselves to exact calculation. Their qualities are known absolutely. They do not vary as one piece of stone or one baulk of timber varies from another. The stone-mason, to make sure of the stability of his walls, relies on a mass of material that is probably unnecessarily great, but the minimum size of beam or stanchion that will carry a given load being exactly calculable, the modern process of design is inevitably one of exploiting the balance of forms and eliminating all but strictly necessary material. In this sense modern architecture has much in common with Gothic architecture, which also evolved by eliminating the superfluous in masonry construction. Gothic architecture, whose soaring pinnacles serve the practical purpose of stabilizing the buttresses which transfer the weight of the roof to the ground, was, it may be noted, a logical result of stone construction, but Classical and Renaissance architecture – the solid wall, pierced by regular windows – was equally so. One suited the aspiring mystical spirit of one age, the other suited the orderly, materialistic spirit of the other – which shows just how different architecture can be in different circumstances without departing from its functionalist basis. That of the modern age is experimental and organic (as distinct from synthetic) in character like the Gothic, but its scientific background pushes it towards an ideal of exactness and order similar to that of the Renaissance.

It is inevitable that the new forms to which modern architecture is introducing us should take some getting used to, and a large part of the disturbing effect that modern architecture has on some people is already disappearing as it becomes more familiar. But reinforced concrete and some of the other synthetic materials present special problems of this kind because they are so far removed from familiar materials. We have the unconscious habit of relating things to what we are already familiar with. We know from repeated experience how strong wood or stone is, for we frequently handle them in other contexts, and when we look at a piece of timber or masonry construction we are immediately satisfied that it is able to do the job that it has to do. But reinforced concrete construction is different; so is a building of steel and glass. We cannot see the steel bars inside the concrete and reassure ourselves that it can safely span several times the distance of the stone lintel it so much resembles, nor can we see the steel stanchions behind a cantilevered store window, so that a building may appear to stand unsafely on a base of glass. It should be realized, however, that the expectation that we shall be able to understand at a glance why a building stands up is a survival of the handicraft age that had disappeared even in the days of William Morris. We cannot see with our eyes why a motor-car travels. We have to accept both the motor-car and modern forms of building construction, such as great cantilevers, both as scientific facts and as typical contemporary objects.

Before we leave the subject of reinforced concrete there is one more aspect of it that should be touched on. It is the question of surface treatment, important because that is one aspect of modern building technique that is still very much in a transitional phase. Concrete walls – thin slabs of reinforced concrete spanning between the structural framework and continuous with it – are a common form of construction, but we know very well how unsatisfactory their external appearance often is. The cleanness and glitter of white walls are satisfying to the modern architect's eye, but in damp or dirty climates few white surfaces survive. They soon become dingy. White walls are not foreign to Britain, which has the successful precedent of Regency stucco buildings. But the smartness of these depends on regular re-painting with expensive oil paint, and in times of financial instability we cannot afford to build in a way that commits us to so much future expenditure on upkeep. Modern architects have made many sad mistakes in using white surfaces that have not lasted, and many now believe that concrete is more satisfactory as a structural material than as a finishing material. There are a number of admirable ways of surfacing a concrete building; coloured tiles for example (as in the Finsbury Health Centre, Plate 30) or panels of glass as in the *Daily Express* building. These materials being non-porous, dirt easily washes off, but they are both expensive. In Italy and Germany they use thin slabs of their local Travertine marble, since they are lucky enough to possess such a material. For buildings in big cities specially textured concrete surfaces are also being developed.

There are other new materials that ought to be mentioned in this chapter, besides steel, concrete, and glass, many of them in their infancy so far as knowledge of their full possibilities is concerned. We are only beginning to explore the possibilities of plastics and of various light metal alloys. Asbestos has a definite place in building; but its fire-resisting qualities were discovered only in 1877. Aluminium has only been used in architecture since about 1890. Plywood, though it is manufactured from the most familiar of all materials, is virtually a new material, as its properties are peculiar to itself.

It is a sheathing material that does not warp even in large sheets, so it need not be divided up into panels and set in grooved frames to allow for possible movements, as ordinary wood must be, which has changed the whole appearance of doors and wall coverings. Plywood is also being used now as a structural material because of the great strength of the sheets when fixed so that they do not bend laterally. Solid timber, too, is being increasingly used, but more scientifically than in the traditional methods of timber construction. Then there is rubber, synthetic wall-boards – the list could be continued indefinitely. And to it could be added the new techniques and the new equipment that have changed the face of building: lifts that made the skyscraper possible – the first lift, referred to as a 'vertical screw railway', was installed in a New York hotel in 1859 – all kinds of electrical machinery; refrigeration and air-conditioning; to say nothing of neon lighting, which now plays so important a part in the design of shop-fronts, restaurants, and cinemas. It would need an encyclopedia to describe them all.

The tendency indeed is for scientific progress to outstrip the ability to apply it. That is what happened in the last century: inventions kept piling up, to the confusion of architect, builder, and public, who had no clear enough architectural philosophy to enable them to use them intelligently. Modern architecture is setting seriously about the task of making something good and coherent out of what science offers.

If a new technique is to be adopted it must be adopted whole. It is of no use trying to cling to the conventions of one world while dabbling in the pleasures of others. There is a moral in the following story. The standard size of bricks, as we have remarked, is such as it is in order that the bricklayer shall be able to hold a brick comfortably in one hand. Not long ago someone thought of introducing larger bricks, so that the work would be done more quickly. But the bricklayer had to use two hands to lift each brick and his whole technique of economical manipulation of brick, trowel, and mortar, which he had used since he was an apprentice, was put out of action; his mate, who handed him up the bricks as the wall rose, found his accustomed job also put out of gear. The innovation was a nuisance not a saving. A differently organized team of workmen with different methods was needed, to make the best of a new material. You cannot tamper with a well-established craft or you lose the best of it. You must develop a new craft when the times demand it. Compromise, like semi-modern architecture, makes the worst of all worlds.

Finally, it may be added that the presentation of modern architecture in this and the previous chapter, first as the product of machinery and then as the product of a number of new building materials, must not be allowed to suggest that it turns its back on everything else. These give the modern architect a special opportunity of bringing buildings into line with contemporary needs and ideas. They offer themselves readily as subjects for experiment, and experiment is the life-blood of architecture. But nothing could be more mistaken than to regard modern architecture as an architecture of steel, plate-glass, and machinery. That would make a cold forbidding world. Warmth and mellowness are qualities people have a right to expect of architecture, and architecture being a visual physical thing, no consciousness of the theoretical rightness of modern architecture would justify it if they were absent. Even if we speak scornfully of the architectural sham represented by, for example, modern Regent Street, a steel skeleton overloaded with period ornament that is both false and unworthy of what architecture can do, the idea behind its richness – even the effect of its richness – as long as it is not accompanied by the same false-ness and vulgarity, is something very much worth having.

People still complain that modern architecture as they see it does not possess enough of the human kind of appeal. This is partly, as I have already said, because it is unfamiliar; but it is partly that modern architecture concentrated to begin with more on achieving the discipline it obviously needed than on the complete range of expression that a mature architecture can afford to use. That it maintains its flexibility is one of the essential characteristics of modern architecture. In this country it has already shown that it is capable of correcting its own faults. For the doctrinaire use of reinforced concrete, which was rightly criticized when its surface was found to wear so badly in damp climates, has already given way to a more careful choice of material. In the next stage in the development of modern architecture the progress was towards greater humanization, through the use of a greater variety of materials, old as well as new, and through the evolution of shapes and textures that produced a richer and more sympathetic character than that which derives from the frigid forms of geometry. Such an emphasis on human as well as mechanical qualities is not a retreat from the ideals of modern architecture. The ideal has always been a human one, and it is natural that the widening of its scope (which is an outcome, really, of maturity) should come after the establishment of its rather revolutionary general principles.

CHAPTER V

THE GROWTH OF THE IDEA

HAVING indicated in the preceding chapters some of the ideas the modern architect has in his mind and some of the materials and methods he has at his disposal, these being jointly responsible for the different appearance of modern architecture from that of earlier generations, we can leave it to the illustrations and the comments accompanying them to show what happens when the ideas and methods are put into practice. For the performance of architecture is infinitely more informative than any amount of theory. But before we look at some examples of recent buildings it may be interesting to see by what stages the ideas behind them gradually established themselves. The early history of modern architecture makes a revealing story,* and one that throws considerable light on the present phase of its development.

Modern architecture did not spring into being all at once. It evolved gradually as it became more and more apparent that a new architecture, based on scientific progress, would satisfy modern needs, both practical and spiritual, in a way that the connoisseur's architecture of the late nineteenth and early twentieth centuries showed no capability of doing. And it did not evolve continuously. During the hundred or so years of its history, signs of its advent appeared in many forms: sometimes as new aesthetic theories, sometimes in an attempt to produce a non-period style of ornament, sometimes simply in the shape of strange new buildings belonging

*It is told more fully than the space in these pages allows by Professor Nikolaus Pevsner in his book, *Pioneers of Modern Design*. See Bibliography.

to no familiar school, the product of original genius that may or may not have realized the nature of the trail it was blazing. It is only in comparatively recent years that these assorted experiments and ideas have coalesced to form a recognizable movement.

We saw in Chapter II how, with the break-up of the eighteenth-century social order, a romantic movement that had started as a dilettante interest in antique and exotic motifs developed into a general revival of all historic styles; how the skilful application of these styles became the whole of architecture, the important jobs that society needed architects to perform (and hence the real architecture of the period) being done by engineers and builders. In the case of the fundamental jobs of planning, in many instances they simply were not done at all. The nineteenth century watched industry become the dominating activity in the national life of most countries without planning for its advent, and we are still suffering from that inertia today.

Various English architects of the early nineteenth century realized that there was something wrong, notably Augustus Welby Pugin, an architect of French descent who worked in England during the thirties and forties. His particular contribution was to realize and expound the importance of structure as the basis of architecture, and he published a book which had great influence, called *Contrasts*, comparing the spirited architecture of the medieval period with the hidebound academic rigidity which was all he saw in the Classic. His enthusiasm for Gothic architecture was bound up with a contemporary religious revival. He advocated a 're-Christianizing' of church architecture. Unfortunately his appreciation of Gothic architecture's structural logic ended in a devotion to the Gothic style as one on which modern buildings might be based. His own designs were something more than mere imitations, but the Gothic revival of which he was the leading exponent ended only in antiquarianism. John Ruskin, the famous critic, was another enthusiastic advocate of Gothic design, its naturalness and spiritual honesty. His writings are full of serious disquisitions on the philosophy of architecture; but his influence, too, did little more than set a fashion for particular medieval styles. These prophets of the Gothic Revival, however, together with Viollet-le-Duc, a French student of medieval life and buildings, and William Morris, whom I have already mentioned, did at least make later progress easier, as they helped to break away from the existing academic tendency to codify architectural design into a system of increasingly rigid formulae. Their limitation was that they could not visualize a new architecture that was not a return to that of some past age.

William Morris's struggle to restore the spirit of handcraftsmanship in the face of the advancing power of machinery has already been referred to. But in spite of this struggle being doomed to failure he has a very important place in the early history of modern architecture. This place is symbolized by the house at Bexley Heath in Kent, which he had built for himself in 1859. It is illustrated in Plate 2, and is known as Red House, being in red brick and tile. The architect was Philip Webb, but the house probably embodies its owner's ideas just as much as its architect's. It was inspired by Morris's enthusiasm for the craftsmanship and character of humble local building, as distinct from the grandiose designs of sophisticated architects. It had many original personal touches, since Webb was an inventive artist, but in general character it might be taken for a slightly unusual farmhouse: and in its time was something quite revolutionary. Its rustic materials – local bricks, tiles, and timber – produced a sensational contrast with the prevalent Italian-style stucco villa and the fashionable architectural ornament imported from medieval Venice or from French chateaux.

By building in so simple a fashion Morris let a new light into the practice of architecture. He was followed by others: notably by Norman Shaw, an architect of great inventiveness, who introduced many new motifs, adapted from past styles, into nineteenth-century English architecture, but who also designed country houses in a romantic rustic manner that carried Philip Webb's experiments in local building methods and materials one stage further; and by C. F. A. Voysey, the most original yet most unassuming of all the new school of domestic architects. Voysey built a number of houses in a purely vernacular fashion, two of which are illustrated in Plate 3. It is difficult to realize how revolutionary such a house as the top one was in 1901. It is only a common type now because of the influence that Voysey and his contemporaries had. Voysey was not trying to devise a modern architecture, nor have the vernacular buildings of this type much in common with modern architecture as we see it today, but he was one of the people who made modern architecture possible because he discarded 'styles' and allowed the job to be done to be the source of style, instead of a historical precedent or accumulation of precedents selected by the architect. He designed in brick, stone, and whitewash, tiles and slates and timber; directly, as a local builder might who had also the eye of an artist to enable him to make something satisfying out of combining his simple walls, roofs, and gables.

Voysey's style was much purer than Norman Shaw's, who, although designing with great freedom and originality, was eclectic; that is, he used any combination of borrowed materials and motifs that he thought helped the effect. Though a healthy influence, his was a sophisticated architecture, like the romantic Swedish architecture exemplified in Stockholm Town Hall which so strongly influenced the eclectic architects of the 1930s.

Coinciding with this new domestic architecture of the 1880s and 1890s was another sign of interest in rural simplicity: the first Garden Suburb. In 1877–80 Norman Shaw designed Bedford Park in west London, a colony of houses placed in gardens amongst trees, and the prototype of all modern suburbs. It is also, alas, the prototype of the endless spread-out of later suburbs which, especially in the period between the two world wars, strangled our towns by cutting them off from the country and nearly killed the idea of the town as a compact aggregation of people living *together*, at the same time killing the art of street design. But at that time it was another breath of nature let into the artificiality of architectural fancy dress. And, together with Ebenezer Howard's later Garden City ideals, it became even more important as an aspect of English domestic architecture that had remarkable influence abroad.

The new English domestic style went from strength to strength. It is only possible to mention the names of some of its leading members, who continued the good work started by Morris, Shaw, and Voysey into the present century: C. R. Ashbee, Baillie Scott, C. R. Mackintosh, George Walton, Ernest Newton, W. R. Lethaby, C. H. Townsend, Guy Dawber, Edwin Lutyens. They built houses for living in, first and foremost. That is their contribution to architectural awakening. Technically of course they still used traditional methods. This revolution in architecture, moreover, important though it was, was confined to domestic buildings. England had to wait a long time before a similar breath of fresh air was let into architecture generally.

Independently, throughout the nineteenth century, the engineers were also experimenting with work that in another way was to help clear the path for modern architecture itself. We have seen how in the early nineteenth century the great English railway and other engineers made the only creative use of the new materials that industry was producing. We have also seen how later in the century French engineers, particularly in the buildings they designed for the great Paris exhibitions of 1867, 1878, and 1889, showed what steel could do. In these years many notable experiments were made, especially in France, in the use of steel and concrete, but they too had little immediate effect on the design of buildings generally.

It is significant that the earliest of all these great exhibition halls was an English one, that designed to contain the Great Exhibition in Hyde Park of 1851, and christened the 'Crystal Palace' (Plate 6). It was in cast iron, not in steel, but had all the inspiring qualities of these great envelopes, which served their purpose of enclosing a huge amount of space beautifully and economically. It was designed by a gardener turned engineer, Sir Joseph Paxton, and historically is more accurately described as the last of the great engineering feats of the early nineteenth century, than as the first monument of a new era. For it set no fashion and caused no immediate revolution. It was only rediscovered as a thing of architectural significance by modern architects in later years. The exhibits it housed included perhaps the most eccentric collection of ornate but tasteless objects in the way of furniture and manufactured articles ever assembled together, and contemporary critics (with the exception of a few whom no one listened to) were blind to the building's beauty. Ruskin hated it, though it embodied a more genuine return to pure and lively structure after the Gothic spirit than anything Pugin or the Gothic Revival produced. It founded no school, yet it is important to us not only because of the simple architectural virtues it and the other great engineering works of the time can now be seen to possess, but because it was an early example of the right use of mass-production. Its whole secret as a building was that it was designed in standard parts:

standard sections of cast iron and standard-size sheets of glass; and the speed and ease with which it was erected was a triumph of industrial organization – a greater triumph indeed than its design. Being the perfect prefabricated building it was equally easily taken down when the Exhibition was over and re-erected on Sydenham Hill to stand for many years as a reproach to architects who would not learn what modern industry could achieve for them.

The rustic or vernacular domestic architecture of Philip Webb, Shaw, and Voysey and the engineering triumphs fifty years earlier of Telford, Brunel, Robert Stephenson, and Paxton are the two English contributions to the growth of the modern architectural idea. After this for many years our story is set elsewhere. For in the same way that Paxton's Crystal Palace had no influence in its time, the revolutionary work of Morris and Voysey, that reached its height at the end of last century, had no influence in the country of its origin beyond its own sphere of small country and suburban houses. The development of modern architecture, though freed from stylistic routine by these pioneers, went no further in England.

On the continent of Europe, as in England, signs of a coming change in architecture appeared independently in different forms. One was a much more conscious attempt than any I have described in England to produce a style that owed nothing to the past. It started in Belgium in the eighties, in a movement led by Henri Van de Velde, which began as discussion among a group of artists about structure and form being the true basis of architecture, much as Ruskin and William Morris had discussed things thirty and forty years earlier. In fact, this movement, which was known as the *Art Nouveau* movement – *Jugendstil* when it spread to Germany – was directly inspired by William Morris. It never got further, however, than the invention of a new kind of ornament. This consisted of an expressive and forceful use of flowing lines, generally based on plant forms, in striking contrast to the rigid geometrical forms of conventional architectural decoration (see Plate 4). In this country the movement is best known in the drawings of Aubrey Beardsley, whose decorative style is a close equivalent to that of *Art Nouveau* decoration, though of course linear where the latter is plastic. But the *Art Nouveau* movement could never form the basis of a new architecture, as it was only concerned with *applied* ornament. Before long it degenerated into fantasy, forgot about the logic of structure – and, lacking any kind of root, died as a result of its own freedom; but it too introduced fresh thought of another kind into the academic sterility of most nineteenth-century architecture.

Art Nouveau had a fashionable success at the Paris Exhibition of 1900. In England it never took strong root, probably because it was not compatible with the already well established Arts and Crafts movement, the latter being based on tradition and the former on novelty. There was one exponent in Britain, however, of considerable importance. This was Charles Rennie Mackintosh, who worked in Glasgow during the last twenty years of the nineteenth century. He has already been mentioned as one of the pioneers of the new vernacular domestic architecture. He is still too little known in his own country, but in Scottish isolation he designed buildings of remarkable originality and having many qualities in common with modern architecture. His most famous work, the School of Art in Glasgow, begun in 1898, is illustrated in Plate 5. Its interior belongs to the school of *Art Nouveau*, as do the interiors he (in collaboration with George Walton) designed and furnished about the same time for a number of Glasgow teashops.

Mackintosh had considerable influence all over Europe, where several exhibitions of his work were held; in fact, at this time all the English experiments already described were bearing fruit on the Continent. Hermann Muthesius, a German for some while resident in England, made the domestic achievements of the English architects known by publishing a book about their work, *Das Englische Haus*, in 1904, which created a sensation in Germany. The casualness and freedom of the work it illustrated, although in many ways an incidental attribute of the rural vernacular ideal, appeared as a quite inspired new architectural philosophy. For on the Continent academic architecture, tight-laced within symmetrical façades, was even more rigidly formal than in England. The Continent had not even had the benefit of the upheaval produced in England by the Gothic Revival. But the *Art Nouveau* movement, even if as a self-contained style it developed only into a rather futile ornamentalism, had prepared the ground for a freer outlook, and the influence of English domestic architecture widened its scope and put it on a more realistic basis. Germany became the centre of much new architectural experiment. In 1907 Henri Van de Velde had been appointed director of the Weimar School of Art. From being concerned with *Art Nouveau* furniture and decoration he turned his attention to the purification of the practical arts (including architecture) and the establishment of new values based on, among other things, the disciplines imposed by new techniques. He and his followers also produced a number of small houses that translated the still rather romantic English ideal into a more rational type. His position gave him considerable influence, and from this time the positive building up of a new architectural style may be said to date, the earlier efforts that I have described being more concerned with breaking down the false academic tradition that had driven architecture away from contemporary life.

Similar efforts were being made at the same time in America, although here the break with academic traditions was confined at first to one type of building, the multi-storey office-block, and one city, Chicago, and made no impression on architecture generally. There had, however, been one earlier pioneer who must not be left out: Henry Hobson Richardson, whose role in America lies somewhere between that of Norman Shaw in England and that of H. P. Berlage (who will be mentioned shortly) on the continent of Europe. Richardson designed in a style reminiscent of the Romanesque, but not in a directly imitative way. He used massively modelled stone walling and semi-circular arcading to produce vigorous geometrical compositions whose sincerity did much to free American building from the trivialities of current antiquarian fashions, and he was responsible for one building, the Marshall Field store in Chicago, completed in 1887, which served more than any other single building of its time as a reminder that good architecture springs directly from honest construction.

The Marshal Field store was of solid stone, but at the time it was built the architect-engineers of Chicago were already venturing into metal-frame construction, which had previously been the subject of but tentative experiments in Britain and France. Most of the pioneer work was done by William Le Baron Jenney, whose ten-storey Home Insurance building was completed in 1885. This was followed by a number of other office buildings, nearly all likewise in Chicago, by various architects, which showed the same appreciation of the regular all-over rhythm that properly belonged to frame buildings, expressed their construction in forthright style, and filled the spaces between the structural framework with large windows to let plenty of light into the offices within. The most notable of these early Chicago skyscrapers were the Leiter and Manhattan buildings (also by Jenney), the Tacoma building (by Holabird and Roche), and the Carson-Pirie-Scott department store (by Louis Sullivan) (Plate 7).

Sullivan's work (mostly done in partnership with Dankmar Adler) was by far the greatest of any produced by the Chicago school of architects. He translated their logical practicality into an architecture of mature artistic rhythms and his skyscrapers of the 1890s, which included also the Wainwright building at St Louis, the Gage building at Chicago, and the Bayard building at New York, were more truly modern than any other American commercial architecture until the 1930s. Sullivan was also a far-sighted architectural philosopher, who saw the architecture of the New World as something itself new in inspiration. There was indeed one moment when, through him, American architecture might have come to lead the modern world: the planning of the great Chicago Exhibition of 1893. It only needed the right kind of impetus to bring a new school of architecture into being, and Sullivan was anxious that this exhibition should provide the architectural occasion America needed. The question was debated, but the exhibition authorities decided to play safe, and selected a grandiose Roman Renaissance architectural scheme for the exhibition buildings. In Sullivan's own words spoken at the time: 'thus architecture died in the land of the free and the home of the brave – in a land declaring its democracy, inventiveness, unique daring, enterprise, and progress. Thus ever works the pallid academic mind, denying the real, exalting the fictitious and false. The damage wrought by the World's Fair will last for half a century from its date, if not longer.' His words came true. A pompous Classic became America's national style, coupled with that horrible invention, Collegiate Gothic, which was devised when her great educational establishments demanded a style distinct from that adopted by big business. America relapsed into the nineteenth century.

The skyscraper, the disappointing child of four grandparents: steel-frame building construction, the electric lift, high city land-values, and American belief in competitive advertising, became for many years no more than a structural skeleton covered with stone designed in some period style – fundamentally there was no difference except one of feet and inches between the Woolworth Building and the Ritz Hotel, and sheer size, from which the skyscraper derived its impressiveness, is not an architectural virtue in itself. The achievements of American architects lay elsewhere. Surprisingly, they competed most successfully with European architects in the skill with which they used period detail for ornamental purposes. Trained in many cases, for reasons of American cultural snobbery, at the *Beaux Arts* school in Paris, American architects eclipsed their own masters in the inventiveness with which banks, libraries, and business houses were decked out with Florentine Renaissance detail, or the magnificence with which a railway terminus was furnished with the costume of an ancient Roman Bath. In the hands of such remarkable men as McKim, Mead, and White this sort of thing was done with astonishing facility; but this too, as we realize today, has little to do with architecture.

One man, however, stood out as an exception: Frank Lloyd Wright, the only native American architect of world significance, and a pupil of Louis Sullivan. Working in the early years of the twentieth century, at the same time as Mackintosh in Scotland, Berlage and Van de Velde in northern Europe, and Otto Wagner in Vienna, he worked out quite independently an original architectural philosophy of his own, going only to the Japanese for foreign inspiration. His houses, which are mostly in or around Chicago, and of which the first was built in 1889, are most striking in being freely planned internally and lit by long horizontal windows beneath widely overhanging eaves. They bear a remarkable contrast to the rigid formal planning of most houses of the period. In other ways his actual building technique and the way he uses natural materials such as wood and stone show many ideas similar to those of William Morris's Arts and Crafts movement, yet he accepted the arrival of the machine as they had never done. Taking his inspiration from the nature of his materials, whether fashioned by hand or machine, he evolved many new and dramatic forms from them. Mistrusting academic rules and sophisticated fashions, he retained his roots in the American soil and the American pioneering tradition, always stressing the importance of a close relationship between buildings and landscape.

Arising from this was his insistence on horizontal lines. He believed that buildings whose main lines lay along the surface of the earth would preserve a proper sense of belonging to it: an idea often justified by the results, yet so typical of the mystical outlook that coloured much of Wright's life and philosophy. His sympathetic approach to nature did not, however, make him a traditionalist; on the contrary, he showed himself a bold innovator at times. Several of his early houses, like that at Woodlawn Avenue, Chicago (1908), were directly inspired by the new potentialities of reinforced concrete; in other houses and at Midway Gardens, Chicago (1914), he based new decorative effects on the use of mass-produced concrete blocks with patterns cast in relief, and his Imperial Hotel, Tokyo (completed 1922), which had floor-slabs balanced over central supports to minimize the effect of earthquake shocks, proved a structural triumph as it was one of the few large buildings in Tokyo to survive the great earthquake of 1923.

But this is taking us ahead of our story. We shall return to Frank Lloyd Wright again. Meanwhile it must be noted that at first his work was largely ignored in his own country, though his influence on modern European architects was, and has since been, profound, the chief intermediary in the first place being the Dutch architect Berlage.

However impersonal much of it is in character, the history of the new architecture is inevitably one of personalities. The pioneer work of individuals comes first, just as the anonymous universal English style of the eighteenth century began with Sir Christopher Wren, Gibbs, Hawksmoor, and William Kent. Our story now returns to central Europe where, in the early years of the twentieth century, a number of great men were independently working their way towards the same goal. Simultaneously with Van de Velde at Weimar in Germany, Otto Wagner and Joseph Hoffman in Austria, H. P. Berlage in Holland, Hans Poelzig and Peter Behrens also in Germany, were among the most notable pioneers. In some cases the advance their work shows was only a new consciousness of the architect's freedom to design rather than imitate, or a new appreciation of simplicity and geometrical form. In others it was a more complete synthesis of means and ends that is recognizable as belonging to the same category as the modern architecture we know. A new architecture was growing up with the new century. What is more, it was at last being applied to other than domestic buildings: to factories, hospitals, schools, the very buildings that belong most typically to modern times.

The next concerted architectural movement was one of the utmost importance for similar reasons. It gave an opportunity for the new ideas to be realistically applied. This was the foundation of the *Deutscher Werkbund* in 1907. It was in a sense a development of the *Art Nouveau* movement of twenty years earlier; but instead of being a movement with all the limitations of art practised for art's sake it was a practical attempt – the first one in history – to get modern artists used by the new industry. The *Deutscher Werkbund* was an association of craftsmen, who arranged exhibitions and studied the problems of applied design. It was therefore also related to the English Arts and Crafts movement fostered by Ruskin and William Morris, the ideals of which had been widely appreciated on the Continent, but it was also fundamentally different in accepting modern industry – that is, machine production – instead of turning its back on it.

It really established the success of the ideas it stood for when Peter Behrens, the most important of the new Continental architects, was appointed, as a result of the *Werkbund* movement, by one of the leading electrical firms in Germany, the A. E. G., both as architect *and as designer of their products*, and even their advertisements. His appointment is a landmark: once more the architect was in his rightful position as the expert on design and master of the machine.

Nevertheless, many of the most notable examples of modern design applied strictly to buildings during this period are private houses, probably because they represented the only architectural type available for free experiment. Adolf Loos, an Austrian, who lived from 1870 to 1933, may be said to be the designer of the first 'modern' house, built round about 1910. This is illustrated in Plate 8. We have seen how the *Art Nouveau* movement, though succeeding in breaking free from the imitation of period styles, only finished by becoming another period style: architecture under its influence was as much a matter of applied ornament as ever. Loos realized this danger, which lies in all new movements, that they become only an end in themselves, and set himself against all ornament, believing that architecture sufficiently well thought-out and designed with sufficient imagination had no need to hide its form under any system of ornament. This creed, again, was not exactly new, but Loos taught it and wrote about it in terms of the conditions that prevailed in his day. The houses he built look somewhat crude to us, but they show remarkable logic and grasp of essentials. Loos, even more than van de Velde, can claim to be the link between the break-away from the old architecture and the building up of a new, without whom the latent good in the *Art Nouveau* movement (which he himself despised) and the conscientious design revival of the *Deutscher Werkbund*, might never have been turned to architectural account. The danger against which Adolf Loos crusaded, of 'modern' design becoming only another applied style, is, as I remarked in the Introduction, an even more real one today. The very confusion that his clear mind sought to avoid has become one of our own greatest handicaps.

Hitherto we have been discussing symptoms and trends, but in the work of Peter Behrens we find modern architecture itself. The example illustrated in Plate 9, the Turbine factory in Berlin, built in 1909, has been called the first piece of modern architecture. It provides a rational solution to a typically modern industrial problem; it makes logical use of modern materials such as steel and glass; it displays with a quite monumental impressiveness the power latent in the simple geometrical shapes that the return to elementary principles of form and technique produced. And it was built in the same year as Selfridge's building in Oxford Street, London. Behrens, incidentally, designed the first modern building in England: a house near Northampton which he was commissioned to design by a Mr Bassett-Lowke in 1926.

Modern architecture had now become more conscious of itself. Instead of individuals working out ideas in isolation or in local groups as in the case of the *Deutscher Werkbund* or Joseph Hoffman's Viennese *Sezession*, it was finding its feet as an international movement, its practitioners in different countries and in different circumstances becoming aware of each other's experiments and being influenced and stimulated by them. But it was not till after the war of 1914–18 that the new architecture attained real status. The special conditions prevalent in 1919 gave it just the stimulus it needed: a new order to be set up in accordance with a new idealism that grew out of the disillusion of the war years; a new housing problem; complete economic and industrial reconstruction, especially in Central Europe, and, again especially in Central Europe, a condition of financial stringency that encouraged strict regard for what was necessary and practical.

Before we come to this period one other contribution to history needs to be recorded. So far we have said nothing about France, except to refer to the great engineering feats that distinguished the Paris Exhibitions of 1867, 1878, and 1889, and Hennebique's experiments in reinforced concrete. France has always been remarkable for engineers of genius, at least since the great Vauban, designer of fortresses for Louis XIV; in fact most engineering and similar inventions of modern times can be traced back to French inventive genius: the motor-car largely to De Dion and Levassor, the photograph partially to Daguerre, and so on. And France can claim that she not only gave modern architecture its favourite structural material, reinforced concrete, but showed how it should be used. It is possible that it was France's very strong academic tradition that prevented her playing an earlier part in the development of modern architecture, a tradition that remained so lively and flexible that it did not give birth to a generation of architectural revolutionaries plotting release from its fetters, as did the sterile academies elsewhere during the latter part of the nineteenth century.

It is during the first two decades of the twentieth century that modern French architects come on the scene, translating the inventions of their own earlier engineers into architectural form. Auguste Perret, in particular, designed a number of reinforced concrete buildings that have been an inspiration to the whole of Europe. His apartment house in the Rue Franklin, Paris, built in 1903, was the first example of reinforced concrete frame construction in architecture. His most epoch-making buildings, all in reinforced concrete, are a garage in the Rue Ponthieu, Paris (1905), a series of dock buildings at Casablanca (1916), and a remarkable church at Le Raincy, near Paris (1925) (Plate 13). Tony Garnier should also be mentioned, especially his *Cité Industrielle*, a model town for 35,000 people designed in 1907 for construction wholly in concrete. Many of the ideas contained in it Garnier was able to realize some years later in his native city of Lille.

Thus at the end of the war of 1914–18, when new social and economic conditions were present to give a new architecture its chance, architects were already equipped with new building techniques from France, a new freedom of planning long ago established in England and America and imported and preserved in Germany and Austria, and in these two latter countries they were even equipped with by no means tentative examples of what a new architecture might actually look like. One further influence should be mentioned, although the whole relationship between the aesthetic ideals of architecture and the development of the other arts is too complicated to be discussed here. This is the influence of Cubism, an immediately pre-war movement in which painters and sculptors concerned themselves with laying bare the geometrical form and structure behind the superficial appearance of things. It is natural that architects should become involved with the ideas on which the Cubist movement was based; indeed Cubism may be said to aim at bringing out the architectural beauty, as distinct from other sources of beauty, in the forms of everything seen; but strangely, except for the single instance of Le Corbusier, whom we shall come back to later, Cubist painting was chiefly allowed to influence modern architecture by way of Holland. A group of Dutch artists, who put forward their ideas in a magazine they designed and published called *De Stijl*, was formed in 1917 under the leadership of the architect Doesberg. It included the painter

78

Piet Mondrian and the architect Oud, and throughout the nineteen-twenties its studies of Cubism and later of abstract art did much to establish the standards of pure geometrical refinement that modern architecture could later claim to have in common with the architecture of ancient Greece and that of England in the late eighteenth century.

CHAPTER VI

AFTER 1918

THE last chapter outlined the growth of modern architecture until immediately after the war of 1914–18. The subsequent period has been one of increasingly rapid architectural change and development, and these are now continuing all round us. At first the most exciting developments took place in Europe, especially in France, Germany, Austria, Holland, and Switzerland. Then the Scandinavian countries joined in, and then Great Britain, the U.S.A., the South American countries, and Italy, roughly in that order.

To represent the developments characteristic of the nineteen-twenties and early nineteen-thirties – a most important formative period – it should be sufficient to say something about the work of two architects, not only because they are the two greatest that modern European architecture has produced, but because they personify two tendencies in which the trend of modern architecture between the wars can be summed up.

These two are Walter Gropius and Le Corbusier. Gropius may be said to be the senior of the two as his earliest works date from about 1911, whereas Le Corbusier is entirely a post-1918 figure. Gropius's earlier works were industrial; they carried on directly the pioneer tradition of Behrens; but his great opportunity came soon after 1919 when Germany, his native country, was undergoing internal reconstruction on a scale that needed the service of architects with far-seeing ideas and the ability to plan for actual social needs, not architects who regarded buildings merely as isolated occasions for putting into practice their personal talent for invention. In the early twenties under the German Republic many enormous housing schemes were planned, following the example of those erected by the socialist municipality of Vienna. They consisted of huge colonies, known as *Siedlungen*, usually complete with schools and shopping centres, the residential part consisting of blocks of flats well spaced out – quite differently from the old-fashioned dark courtyard plan which has given such a bad name to large-scale official housing in many countries – and carefully aligned to make the most of the sun. The gardens between the blocks were for the common use of tenants, though sometimes small private plots were provided as well, and each flat had a spacious balcony of the kind that is now provided for all modern flats. The numerous *Siedlungen*, notably those round the outskirts of Berlin and at Frankfurt and elsewhere, constitute one of the greatest building schemes in history, and provided wonderful experience for the modern architects to whom they were entrusted.

Gropius himself designed several of these housing schemes, but his fame chiefly rests on another achievement: the celebrated *Bauhaus* at Dessau, which was a sort of university of design. Henri Van de Velde's influence as director of the Weimar Art School has already been mentioned. In 1919 Gropius was appointed to succeed Van de Velde and was given the opportunity of remodelling the school according to plans of his own. In 1925 the school was moved to Dessau, where Gropius was invited by the Town Council to design a great group of buildings, including the school itself with all necessary living accommodation, a labour exchange, and a housing colony. Here it flourished until the advent of the Nazi regime in 1933, when it was closed down. At the same time Gropius, who had resigned from the *Bauhaus* in 1928 to concentrate on his own housing work, left the country.

The idea on which the *Bauhaus* School was based was

partly the importance of unity between all the arts and partly the importance of industrial production as the biggest factor in modern design. Gropius's aim was, in his own words, that of 'realizing a modern architectural art which, like human nature, should be all-embracing in its scope. Within that sovereign federative union all the different "arts" (with the various manifestations and tendencies of each) – every branch of design, every form of technique – could be coordinated and find their appointed place. Our ultimate goal, therefore, was the complete and inseparable work of art, the great building, in which the old dividing-line between monumental and decorative elements would have disappeared for ever.'*

One means of achieving this aim was to produce in the various departments of the school a high quality of standard designs for mass production: units for prefabricated building as well as furniture, textiles, and so on, that would meet all the technical, aesthetic, and commercial demands of contemporary conditions. With this last point in view, that is, in order to keep the students of design working in relation to the machines that would have to make their products, manual instruction was the basis of tuition, 'not', to use Gropius's own words again, 'an end in itself, or with an idea of turning it to incidental account by actually producing handicrafts' (this, of course, is the fundamental difference between the *Bauhaus* movement and William Morris's Arts and Crafts movement), 'but as providing a good all-round training for hand and eye, and being a practical first step in mastering industrial processes. The *Bauhaus* workshops were really laboratories for working out practical new designs for present-day articles and improving models for mass production.' The

*Quoted from *The New Architecture and the Bauhaus*, by Walter Gropius (translated by P. Morton Shand). London: Faber and Faber, 1935.

actual building of the new school at Dessau, in which students and teachers cooperated, was also a valuable practical experience.

The *Bauhaus* rapidly acquired wide influence, not only because designs which it produced were adopted for mass production by industrial concerns, but because it became the intellectual centre and fount of inspiration for the whole new architectural movement that was spreading fast through Central Europe. The unanswerable logic of Gropius's own ideas was supplemented by the actual work of students and teaching staff, who included some of the best artists and designers in Germany, many of whom the reputation of the *Bauhaus* had brought from other countries.

Gropius's own architecture, as exemplified in the *Bauhaus* buildings (see Plate 11), is rational to the point of extreme – almost forbidding – severity; but so thoroughly and rhythmically planned, with every part in perfect coordination, as to give the whole a sort of nobility that a more fanciful style seldom achieves.

This quality of rectitude is in striking contrast to the romantic, poetic quality we find in the work of Le Corbusier. Le Corbusier is Swiss by origin and his real name is Charles Edouard Jeanneret; but he has lived so long in Paris and such a large part of his work has been done in France that he may reasonably be regarded as a French architect. The real nature of his work is the subject of much confusion, as his character as a propagandist so often seems to differ from his character as an architect. His name, because of his writings, became closely associated with the idea of 'functionalism', yet his buildings are much less functionalist than those of Gropius. Similarly, his writings are full of social philosophy and of plans for a new architectural Utopia, yet Gropius's buildings did much more to relate architecture to immediate social needs, Le Corbusier's being more personal and impulsive. Although he is always true to his enthusiasm for modern technique, it has been aptly said that he designs rather than builds. His best work shows a poetic and imaginative use of geometrical forms, inspired originally by Cubism.

Another contrast that illustrates still further the conflicting yet complementary tendencies which emerged as modern architecture established itself simultaneously in different parts of the world, is the contrast between the work of Le Corbusier and that of Frank Lloyd Wright, the American architect who, as already described in the last chapter, had long been fighting a solitary battle in his own country. Wright builds consciously in sympathy with nature; Le Corbusier in defiance of it. He exploits the surprising, and at first sight unnatural, things modern construction will do. Unlike Wright, whose buildings lie close to the ground, Le Corbusier's often stand up on pillars as near as possible floating in the air, dissociated from the earth. Further, the contrasting nature of their work illustrates the two dangers that modern architecture tends to be led into. Le Corbusier's romantic geometry, disciplined by Cubism, tends to exhaust itself in sterile abstraction of form, or in a renewal of academic formulae. It has this tendency in common with the more doctrinaire modernism of the *Bauhaus* School. In contrast, Wright's more 'natural' architecture tends to escape from technical and social problems into art-and-crafty idealism. The ideal of course is a fusion of these two tendencies: an architecture that is free and natural without being unworldly, and in tune with the mechanical world without being inhumanly exclusive.

I have not the space to discuss individually the work of other architects of the post-1918 generation; though some examples are shown in the illustrations and described in the notes about them in Chapter VIII. Modern architecture at this time became fully established as an idea, even if its products had not achieved a very advanced degree of maturity or refinement.

Among the architects who helped it to become so should be named: Gropius, Erich Mendelsohn, Bruno Taut, Hans Poelzig, Ernst Mai, and Mies van der Rohe in Germany; Le Corbusier, André Lurçat, and Beaudouin and Lods in France; J. J. P. Oud, J. B. van Loghem, Mart Stam, J. Duiker, Brinkman, and Van der Vlugt and Van Eesteren in Holland; Alvar Aalto in Finland; Gunnar Asplund and Sven Markelius in Sweden; Josef Gocar, Bohuslav Fuchs, Havlicek, and Honzig in Czechoslovakia; Fred Forbat, Marcel Breuer, and Molnar Farkas in Hungary; Josef Frank, Otto Strnad, and Ernst Plischke in Austria; Karl Moser, Alfred Roth, Werner Moser, Haefeli, and Steiger in Switzerland; the Syrkus's in Poland; Jose Luis Sert in Spain; Malevich in Russia; Richard Neutra and William Lescaze in the United States of America; Wells Coates, Maxwell Fry, Owen Williams, Joseph Emberton, T. S. Tait, Connell, Ward and Lucas, B. Lubetkin, and F. R. S. Yorke in England.

Several of these are now working in other countries than those they then belonged to, which brings us to a factor that cannot be omitted in surveying the history of modern architecture: the influence of politics on the course of architecture. Modern ideas in design have become identified with progressive ideas politically and have, therefore, been looked upon with disfavour by anti-progressive political dictatorships. Germany is the most striking case in point. It was in a way natural that modern architecture should have been regarded as incompatible with Nazism; not, as the dictatorships themselves suggested, because it was a 'Bolshie' architecture devised by Reds or by Jews, but simply because it is rational and matter-of-fact, by-passing as architecturally irrelevant the pomp that would make architecture a useful medium for the glorification of the State. Furthermore, it is international in scope, ignoring the very distinctions that nationalism tries to emphasize – the modern architecture of pre-Nazi Germany could in no obvious sense be described as Germanic. Finally it was bound to be resented as one of the most striking creations of the short-lived German democratic republic and be stamped out with all possible force by the Nazi regime that succeeded it.

There are probably other reasons why the Nazi regime in particular disliked the flourishing new architecture that it found when it came into power. For example the concentrated planning of the new housing schemes offered ideal opportunity for the organization of a secret opposition; the Nazi policy of cottage housing in a traditional style is also one of decentralization of the working class. But we are not concerned with the political aspect of architecture; we are only concerned with its results when they are part of the history of architectural development.

The period of greatest achievement for the modern architects in Germany was between 1925 and 1933. In those years Germany was proud to be the centre of a new culture more lively and more promising than Europe had seen for 150 years. The advent of Nazism in 1933 brought that episode to an end. The official architecture of Nazism was a kind of simplified classical, sometimes effective because of its monumental scale but culturally a return to the age of Bismarck. This date is not only important because it marks the end, for a time, of modern architecture in Germany, but because it marks the beginning of a great exodus of modern architects out of Germany, a considerable factor in the spread of modern architectural ideas elsewhere. If they were of Jewish extraction, or if they had been associated with progressive politics of any kind, even the most distinguished modern architects were expelled from Germany. If they were blameless in this way they were equally effectively driven out, as it was made impossible for them to work.

During the years immediately following, some of the best modern architecture was being done in Austria and particularly in Czechoslovakia, but later the modern architects from these countries became refugees in their turn. This alarming and, for its victims, tragic state of affairs was not, however, a threat to the survival of modern architecture itself; the speed at which it spread and the security with which it became absorbed into the life of many nations far outweighed any temporary local eclipse. It was Germany's loss, not architecture's. The exodus from the Nazi-dominated countries was particularly beneficial, first to Britain and then to the U.S.A. Gropius himself came to work in England in 1934, and the benefit the young English architects derived from his mature experience is incalculable. Erich Mendelsohn and Marcel Breuer did the same. In the late thirties they all three moved on to America, where Gropius became Professor of Architecture at Harvard University, which he made into a powerful centre of progressive architectural ideas. Another German refugee who settled in America was Mies van der Rohe. His precise, logical studies in pure geometry have achieved a strong following and must be returned to in the next chapter.

The case of Italy between the two world wars was oddly different from that of Germany. Italian Fascism found no recently established new architecture that it felt bound to stamp out as representing the preceding regime. There was no interregnum in Italy between the pre-1918 order and the Fascist order, and Fascism, anxious to advertise itself as a movement of youth and progress, gave its official blessing to the new architecture. This attitude was in any case more natural because of the precedent of Futurism, a pre-war Italian politico-artistic movement of considerable influence in European artistic circles, led by the writer and painter Marinetti. This group was also Fascist in belief. One of its prominent members, Antonio Sant' Elia, the most promising modern architect Italy had produced, was killed in 1916 when only 28 years old.

Fascist Italy, therefore, proclaimed modern architecture as its own. But it was hardly to be expected that a government that officially adopted modernism simply because it was progressive would automatically produce good modern buildings: they do not come from wishing to be up-to-date, nor are they fitted to serve the purpose of glorifying an authoritarian regime. The official architecture of Italian Fascism was only superficially modern. In spirit it was not unlike the official German architecture, though less bound to the clichés of imperial pomp and more advanced technically. But the position in Italy did mean that such genuinely modern architects as Italy possessed were allowed to work freely instead of being denied all opportunity as in Germany, and Italian architects produced some admirable buildings which, overshadowed by the rather showy modernity of her official buildings, have never been given the credit as serious contributions to the mass of European modern architecture which is their due. How sound their instincts were is shown by the speed with which Italy swept into a leading place among the countries producing good modern architecture after the war of 1939–45.

In Russia, the third country where the ideas of those in control have been imposed on architectural style, the pendulum has swung through extreme distances. In the years following the Revolution, architecture partook of the revolutionary fervour and Russia was the happy hunting ground for all experimental creeds. Modern architecture flourished – at least in ideas. Huge socialist building programmes provided the opportunity, and a large quantity of modern buildings of excellent intention but uncertain technical quality were put up, in many cases by distinguished European architects (among whom was Le Corbusier himself) who were invited to Russia to assist the great programme of socialist reconstruction. But this phase lasted only a few years. After about 1928 Russia turned her back on the new architecture that Europe had been struggling to produce in the face of just those difficulties, absence of planning legislation and absence of community of aim, that Russia was in the strongest position to surmount, and adopted a heavy neo-classical style depressingly like that favoured in Nazi Germany. In many ways, indeed, she went back still further: to the use of the classical orders in the old simple bourgeois way. A tragic instance is Moscow's huge new underground railway system. From the engineering point of view it is a superb achievement; but the stations, vulgarly ornate in neo-classical style, faced in expensive marbles, show official Russian taste at its very worst.

This strange reaction is difficult to explain, so complex, obscure, and hard for us to understand are the various factors that have been at work moulding Russian life ever since the Revolution. Partly the explanation is technical. It was a reaction against the technical failure of the early modern architecture, which was put up in a hurry, without skilled labour, often in unsuitable materials and certainly without the backing of a highly organized – and highly mechanized – building industry such as modern architecture in Europe had grown up with. Disillusioned by the poor quality of their modern buildings from the point of view of finish, weather resistance, and even stability, the Russians turned to the more tried and solid methods of traditional building and the academic styles associated with them. But it was probably also a matter of propaganda and prestige. Architecture was required to serve as a symbol of the successful establishment of the new

regime, and to the impressionable peasant, for example, pay-
ing a visit to Moscow, palatial stone buildings decked with
rows of sturdy columns were more convincing evidence of
the progress of the Five Year Plan than modern buildings of
whatever quality, which for him had no associations with
prosperity and security; nothing to make him proud of his
share in them. Architectural progress, that is to say, could
not be allowed to move faster than popular education.

The influence of politics on the architecture of Europe in
the nineteen-twenties and thirties – an influence that in the
Russian case has continued to this day – is recorded here as
a matter of history. It may be labelled unfortunate in the
light of its immediate effect in the countries concerned, but
architecture, nevertheless, cannot escape from politics, since
it is a social service as well as an art. This is not to say that
modern architecture should tie itself to one particular party –
it values its scientific detachment too much for that – though
it is natural that modern architecture should be associated
with progressive movements and find itself in antagonism to
the forces of conservatism, particularly when it comes up
immediately against political issues in matters like housing
and regional planning, against the vested interests that thrive
on ribbon development, against the economics of land values,
and against the restrictions of petty legislation. And the
architect in his capacity of planner is naturally very conscious of how many of our ills are attributable to lack of
planning, foresight, and purpose. The danger is that many
more narrowly architectural problems that are still awaiting
attention may be sacrificed to architecture's newly resumed
social responsibilities. These latter, however, obviously provide the only means by which the architect's dream of a
better world has any chance of being realized.

I have not discussed planning much in this book because
I set out chiefly to explain the unfamiliar appearance of

modern architecture. This is bound up with planning in the sense that the plan of a building is the whole basis of its design; indeed, the pioneer modern architects whose work I have described have put their ideals into practice as much by applying logic and scientific methods to the planning of buildings as by applying it to their structural form. But the technique of planning, once we have recognized its underlying importance, is not our subject. Strictly the architect is as much a planner as anything else, and the orderliness that he can produce in place of confusion by making sure that ends are exactly suited by means is the greatest service he can offer society.

To get back to our story of the spread of modern architectural ideas and the forms in which they expressed themselves in different parts of the world, an important event of the nineteen-thirties was the emergence of the Scandinavian countries as the scene of much activity and many instructive experiments. These countries were late in contributing anything of their own to the new architectural movement, probably because its first revolutionary impetus had little appeal for them. Their own native tradition, not having become debased during an industrialized nineteenth century, was in no need of drastic measures to revive it. Nevertheless it was in Scandinavia that an event took place at this time which did more than anything else to arouse public interest in modern architecture: the Stockholm Exhibition of 1930 (see Plate 15), for which the architect was Gunnar Asplund. Previously modern buildings had been seen only in the form of isolated structures that inevitably looked stranger than they really were when surrounded by the mixed architectural styles of the average city street, but at Stockholm a whole sequence of buildings – as it might be a whole new quarter of a town – was designed and laid out in a consistently modern style, and the public, walking among them, was given its first glimpse of modern architecture not as a new fashion in design but as a newly conceived environment.

From then onwards, modern architecture in Scandinavia forged ahead rapidly, outrivalling the picturesque style exemplified by Ostberg's Stockholm Town Hall (completed in 1923), which had become so popular with romantically-minded architects in England and elsewhere, and the more sophisticated neo-classical style of the equally admired Ivar Tengbom. But the somewhat doctrinaire puritanism typical of Central Europe at this time, and especially associated with the *Bauhaus*, was modified, in Sweden particularly, by a strong craft tradition. A preference for natural materials (Sweden contributed but little to the technical experiments on which modern architecture had thrived in other countries), the modest domestic scale on which even the larger buildings were conceived, and a sympathetic way of handling materials gave the Swedish brand of modern architecture a more human character which appealed strongly to those who preferred the break with the past softened by a charm of manner generally associated only with period reminiscence. This very charm carried with it the obvious danger that it might come to be valued above the more essential architectural qualities.

The strength of the Swedish architecture of the nineteen-twenties and thirties lay in its happy relationship with the landscape (or with the street scene in the case of town buildings), in its craftsmanlike attention to detail, and in the fact that it had official support. In most other countries modern architecture had to fight against official conservatism; in Scandinavia, Government and local authorities often took the lead in sponsoring progressive architectural ideas, thereby strengthening the whole movement and translating the description 'municipal' almost into a guarantee of quality and enlightenment instead of, as elsewhere, a synonym of dreary conventionality or empty rhetoric. As a result Sweden especially, with her instinct for using materials well and her serious sense of social values, began setting an example to all Europe of the way modern architecture could solve such different problems as the housing of industrial workers and the mass production of elegant household furniture.

Finland, tougher and more hard-living, did not wholly share the tendencies that gave the architecture of the rest of Scandinavia a character of its own, but it produced at this time one outstanding architect, Alvar Aalto, whose bold use of new methods of construction (especially reinforced concrete), combined with his original and imaginative handling of Finland's traditional raw material, timber (notably in the Finnish pavilions that he designed at the Paris Exhibition of 1937 and the New York World Fair of 1939) made him the man to whom many of the younger European architects looked to show how modern architecture might, without compromising with its principles, achieve the depth and richness and sense of human values also associated with the peculiar genius of Frank Lloyd Wright.

In America Wright was still a solitary figure, though building actively and tireless in spreading his gospel of an 'organic' architecture, by which is meant one that eschews formality, being the product of an instinctive rather than an intellectual process, and claims that the architect's chief inspiration should be the *genius loci* and the nature of materials. Taliesin a id Taliesin West, Wright's summer and winter homes in Wisconsin and the Arizona desert (Plate 38), established in 1911 and 1938 respectively, were also the home, after 1932, of the Taliesin Fellowship, a community in which Wright worked, surrounded by young men who combined the roles of devoted disciple and office apprentice with labour on the Taliesin buildings, and learnt with their own hands to put Wright's architectural precepts into practice. Wright produced a vast variety of work, ranging from huge planning projects to more of his unconventionally planned but very liveable-in houses. He also entered the field of industrial architecture with his Johnson Company administrative building at Racine. Its hall of slender concrete columns rising to a luminous glass ceiling aroused much interest and admiration and showed that Wright was equally at home with new and with traditional materials.

But the mass of American architecture continued in its old derivative courses, and even when isolated buildings of modern design began to appear they were regarded by most people simply as a new fashion – the latest from Europe – that had arrived to compete with New England Georgian and banking-house Florentine. Only in California did the new conception of architecture find real scope. The Pacific coast had a tradition of spacious, casually planned, single-storey houses dating from pioneer days, mostly timber built and inspired by the mild climate to ignore the conventional barrier between indoors and out. This tradition was carried on in spirited fashion by a number of modern architects, of whom the most prominent was Richard Neutra, an Austrian by origin whose special forte was the studied relationship of building to landscape.

His were mostly private houses for wealthy clients, and therefore but little concerned with the great problems of the modern world that the new techniques of architecture were so well equipped to solve, and of which an expanding country like the United States should have been specially conscious. The first enterprise of this kind in which modern design played a noteworthy part was the great experiment in land reclamation and development known as the T.V.A. (Tennessee Valley Authority) scheme. The many engineering works – dams, power stations, and so on – and their equipment, though conceived without architectural pretensions, showed a consistent and forthright style of design, the result of engineers and architects collaborating as anonymous members of a building team. Here was a specifically American contribution: the application of modern design in a pioneering, socially significant context.

The nineteen-thirties also saw a gradual improvement in the treatment of the tall office building, the typical American city structure: a simplification of line and detail stemming from a new appreciation of the beauty latent in smooth upward-reaching lines and the repetition of identical window-units. Among the most distinguished examples were the *Daily News* building in New York (by Raymond Hood and John Mead Howells, 1930) and the Savings Society building in Philadelphia (by Howe and Lescaze, 1932) (see Plate 20). Two other promising developments were the construction of Rockefeller Center, New York (completed 1940), a group of no less than fourteen tall buildings planned round a piazza, showing that modern cities could plan on more comprehensive lines than those of the single building lot, and the setting up, also in New York, of the Museum of Modern Art in a building, designed by Philip Goodwin and Edward D. Stone, not unworthy of its purpose.

Politics in Europe, and the lingering eclecticism of America, threw special responsibility in the nineteen-thirties on Great Britain. Britain has played no part in our story since the time of Voysey's and Mackintosh's influence thirty years earlier. But about 1930 the new European architecture that these men helped to make possible found its way back across the Channel. At first only a handful of British architects were propagating what was essentially a European idea, but soon the handful had grown to many. England for a time became the headquarters of modern architecture, a position she was helped to achieve by the presence of several eminent refugee architects from Nazi Germany – among them

Gropius, Mendelsohn, and Breuer – whose migration first to England and then to America has already been referred to.

At first private houses constituted a very large proportion of the total number of modern buildings. It was natural that this should be so, both in Britain and elsewhere, since nearly all new movements, artistic and otherwise, are fostered at first by private individuals. The good fortune of modern German architecture in being linked almost from the beginning with industrial undertakings and the great municipal housing schemes was unusual; so was that of the Scandinavian in having the backing of public authorities. In Britain the first opportunities that modern architecture had were offered by a limited intelligentsia who were in touch with developments on the Continent and recognized the germ of a new culture in the modern buildings that were being put up in France and Germany. A private house, moreover, does not represent a very large amount of capital sunk in an unusual enterprise, and its owner is responsible only to himself. But modern architecture's identification in its early days almost exclusively with houses was not altogether to its advantage. For the private house, as I pointed out in an earlier chapter, is the one type of building whose function has not changed fundamentally since a hundred years ago. It provided a useful field for experiment, but until the architect had experience in applying modern methods to something that was more typically a modern problem, he could hardly hope that his art would attain maturity in any sense, or rise to proper social usefulness, and this position was not reached till just before 1939 when the outbreak of war put an end to all civilian building.

Another cause of modern architecture's relatively slow progress in Britain has already been mentioned: the traditional conservatism of the various Government authorities. Modern architecture in England had not the benefit of official

THE BEGINNINGS OF
MODERN ARCHITECTURE

824–1828. St Katharine's Docks, London, by Thomas Telford. Typical of
he simple but noble engineer's architecture of this time.

1859. Red House. Bexley Heath, Kent, designed by Philip Webb for William Morris. It appeared as a startling contrast to the regulars Italian-style stucco villas of the mid Victorian period.

Top, 1901. The Pastures, North Luffenham, Rutland, a typical country house by C. F. A. Voysey, returning once more to native craftsmanship and materials.

Bottom, 1899. The sitting-room in the house Voysey designed for himself: The Orchard, Chorley Wood.

3

1893. An *Art Nouveau* interior: the staircase hall of a house in the Rue Turin, Brussels, by Victor Horta.

898–1899. Glasgow School of Art, by Charles Rennie Mackintosh. A
building remarkably in advance of its time.

Top, the Crystal Palace, designed by Sir Joseph Paxton for the Great Exhibition, Hyde Park, London, 1851, photographed as re-erected afterwards at Sydenham.

Bottom, the *Galerie des Machines*, designed by Cottancin for the Paris Exhibition of 1889.

Department store, Chicago, 1899–1906, by Louis Sullivan.

Top, 1910. A house by Adolf Loos in Vienna. It looks a little crude now,
but in its day its severe character had a very healthy influence.

Bottom, 1901. A house at Oak Park, Illinois, by Frank Lloyd Wright,
America's pioneer modern architect.

1909. A factory in the Huttenstrasse, Berlin, by Peter Behrens. It has been called the first modern building.

9

1916. Reinforced concrete airship hangars at Orly, France, by Eugène Freyssinet.

PIONEER WORK
BETWEEN THE WARS IN EUROPE, AMERICA, AND BRITAIN

Top, the *Bauhaus* at Dessau, Germany, by Walter Gropius, 1925: Gropius's famous school of design.

Bottom, one section of the great Siemensstadt housing scheme, near Berlin, by Walter Gropius, 1929.

Top, a reinforced concrete bridge at Valtschiel, Switzerland, by Robert Maillart, 1925–1926.

Bottom, a row of small houses at Stuttgart, by the Dutch architect, J. J. P Oud, 1927.

12

Reinforced concrete church at Le Raincy, France, 1925, by Auguste Perret.

Top, a house at Garches, near Paris, by Le Corbusier and Pierre Jeanneret, 1927.

Bottom, the staircase hall of the Villa Savoye at Poissy, by Le Corbusier and Pierre Jeanneret, 1929–1931.

14

The Stockholm Exhibition of 1930: top, the building
displaying hotel and office equipment and leather
goods; bottom, a restaurant interior. Gunnar Asplund,
architect.

15

Paimio Tuberculosis Sanatorium, Finland by Alvar Aalto 1932 · view from the south-west.

16

An elementary school at Villejuif, a suburb of Paris, by Andre Lurçat, 1932.

Top, Bergpolder flats, Rotterdam, by Brinkman and Van der Vlugt, 1934, the western side.

Bottom, flats at Doldertal, Zurich, Switzerland, by A. and E. Roth and Marcel Breuer, 1936.

18

The Old Age Pensions Institute in Prague, by Havlicek and Honzik. 1934: approach from the centre of the city.

Left, Daily News building, New York, by Raymond Hood and John Mead Howells, 1930.

Right, Philadelphia Savings building, by Howe and Lescaze, 1932.

Ministry of Education, Rio de Janeiro, by Oscar Niemeyer and others, 1937.

Chemical factory at Beeston, Nottinghamshire, by Sir E. Owen Williams. 1931.

Arnos Grove underground station, by Adams, Holden, and Pearson, 1932.

Bexhill Entertainments Pavilion, by Mendelssohn and Chermayeff, 1936: a view along the sun-deck which faces the sea, taken from outside the main staircase.

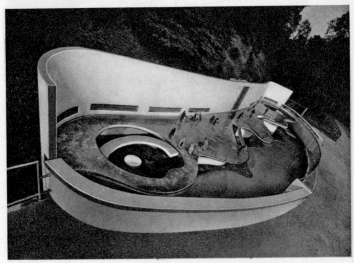

Top, Kensal House, 1936: a working-class housing-scheme in Ladbroke Grove, London, by E. Maxwell Fry working in conjunction with a committee of architects consisting of Robert Atkinson, C. H. James, and G. G. Wornum and with Elizabeth Denby as housing consultant. The east front of the main block.

Bottom, the Penguin Pool at the Dudley Zoo, 1938, by Tecton.

An all-timber country house at Halland, Sussex, by Serge Chermayeff, 1938. Top, the garden side, facing south, containing the windows of all the principal rooms; bottom, the living-room, looking through the sliding windows on to the terrace.

Electricity showrooms in Regent Street, London, by E. Maxwell Fry, 1938: a night view from the pavement.

28

Peter Jones's department store, Sloane Square, London, by William Crabtree (in association with Slater and Moberly and Prof. C. H. Reilly), 1936–1939.

29

The Finsbury Borough Health Centre, by Tecton, 1938: one of the two wings containing clinics and offices.

SOME REPRESENTATIVE MODERN BUILDINGS IN EUROPE, AMERICA, AND BRITAIN

Pirelli building, Milan, by Gio Ponti, 1960.

Top, railway terminus at Rome, 1950, by Calini, Castellazzi, Fadigatti, Montuori, Pintonello, and Vitellozzi: the main public hall.

Bottom, civic centre, Säynätsalo, Finland, by Alvar Aalto, 1951.

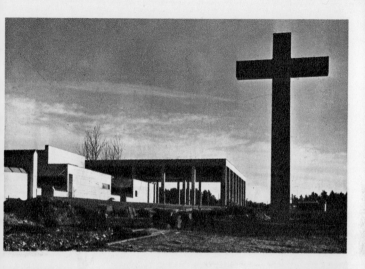

Top, crematorium outside Stockholm, by Gunnar Asplund, 1940.
Bottom, flats at Grondal, Stockholm, by Backstrom and Reinius, 1946.

Top, flats at Marseilles, by Le Corbusier, 1947–1952.
Bottom, Pilgrimage chapel at Ronchamp, France, by Le Corbusier, 1955.

Business training college at Heidelberg, Germany, by F. W. Kraemer, 1957

35

Top, house at Cohasset, Massachusetts, by Walter Gropius and Marcel Breuer, 1939.

Bottom, interior of living-room, house at Six Moon Hill, Boston, Mass., by the Architects' Collaborative, 1951.

House in Colorado, by Richard J. Neutra, 1946.

Taliesin West, near Phoenix, Arizona, by Frank Lloyd Wright, 1938.

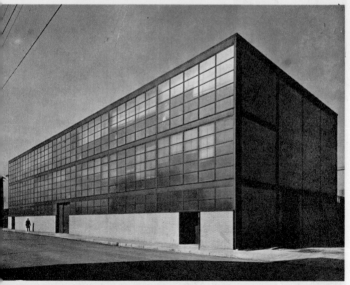

Top, opera house at Stockbridge, Mass., by Saarinen, Swanson, and Saarinen, 1947.

Bottom, Metals and Minerals Research Building, one of a group of buildings designed by Mies van der Rohe for the Illinois Institute of Technology, Chicago, 1953.

Lever building, New York, by Skidmore, Owings, and Merrill (chief designer Gordon Bunschaft), 1952.

Top, residential neighbourhood at Pedregulho, on the
outskirts of Rio de Janeiro,
by Affonso Reidy, 1949–
1954: part of the primary
school, showing coloured
tile decoration.

Bottom, President's palace
at Brasilia, the new capital
of Brazil, by Oscar Nie-
meyer, 1958.

Infants' School at St Albans, by C. H. Aslin, Hertfordshire county architect
1951: top, classrooms from the south; bottom, interior of classroom.

Housing in Pimlico, Westminster, by Powell and Moya, 1950.

South Bank Exhibition, London, 1951: Sir Hugh Casson, Director of Architecture. Left, Waterloo Gate, by Fry, Drew and Partners. Right, main concourse laid out by H. T. Cadbury Brown with Transport building by Arcon; Royal Festival Hall in the background.

44

Royal Festival Hall, London, by Robert H. Matthew, architect to the London County Council, J. L. Martin, deputy architect, Edwin Williams. and Peter Moro. 1951.

Figure ... Round ... Seaside Wales ... by the Architects' Co-operative Partnership, 1951

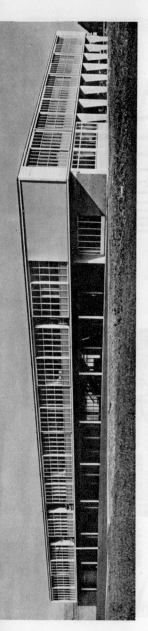

Top, secondary school at Cranford, Middlesex, by Denis Clarke-Hall, 1953.
Bottom, offices at Poole, Dorset, by Farmer and Dark, 1954.

Right, Gatwick airport, Sussex, by Yorke, Rosenberg, and

Left, flats at Roehampton, by the London County Council

encouragement, as it had in the Scandinavian countries, for example, and in Germany before 1933 and in Czechoslovakia before 1938. On the contrary, the official architecture was the most backward, and not only did this apply to the work done by the official architectural offices, but also to work done by private architects for municipal and other authorities.

The former represent a very important recent development in the organization of the architectural profession, in Britain especially. After 1918 public offices grew rapidly in size until quite a large proportion of the buildings put up all over the country were designed in one of them, such as the Office of Works, the London County Council, and so on; or else in architectural departments run by industrial and other concerns. This was all to the good in many ways, but it raised the problem of how the freedom and personal enthusiasm that the creation of good architecture needs could be preserved within a bureaucratic system, a problem still only partially solved. The danger is partly that, promotion being largely by seniority, it is the 'safe', industrious civil servant who attains the position of responsibility, and shapes the mould into which all the official architecture should be cast rather after his own image; and partly that the subdivision of work into an infinite number of specialized tasks means that the architects are not personally responsible for any one building. The result is that the work becomes stereotyped and lacking in inspiration. The remedy seems to be some group system of work, whereby a small number of architects are solely responsible for everything pertaining to one building until it is finished, preserving the essential enthusiasm and unity of intention.

In the case of buildings designed by private architects for official purposes – town halls, public libraries, and so on – another problem presents itself. A town hall is partly a ceremonial building and needs to have a dignity that will form a fitting background for ceremonial. It must also express in some way the dignity of the State. But architecture expresses qualities like these by association; the soaring pinnacles of a cathedral have associations with spiritual values and the columned portico of a palace suggests temporal power, but modern architecture is too new a growth yet to have any associations of this sort. This is not to say that dignity is not compatible with modern design, but as it is a psychological as well as an architectural attribute of a building it must largely be brought to it by the spectator, who still only sees technical perfection and functional efficiency in modern buildings, not dignity. The extreme pomp of monumental buildings is not perhaps a character a democratic age demands, but we shall come to appreciate in time the special form of dignity produced by orderliness and spacious planning. The great housing scheme boasting these qualities, and incorporating as it does its own schools and community centres, can claim to represent this age as aptly as the religious power and mysticism of the fourteenth century or the aristocratic arrogance of the seventeenth were represented by the typical architecture of those periods. Meanwhile our civic life in the 1930s preferred to clothe itself in Georgian dress, with fashionable trimmings imported from Sweden or elsewhere. It was effective in an easy way, but we want something more than scenery from architectural design.

There were at this time a few exceptions to official architecture's general conservatism. Some education authorities, notably in Cambridgeshire and Yorkshire, gave modern architects a chance of showing what schools might be like in a world less bound to the outward forms of tradition; in London the Borough of Finsbury distinguished itself by making the word 'municipal' mean something inspiring instead of depressing (one of Finsbury's enterprising municipal buildings is illustrated on Plate 30), and the Royal

Zoological Society, which can appropriately be referred to here although it is strictly a private organization, gave the firm of young architects called Tecton the opportunity of first demonstrating how exciting and dramatic as well as efficient modern architecture can be. Some of their zoo buildings, both in Regent's Park and at Whipsnade, were among the first examples of modern architecture to become well known to the English public.

But there was one semi-public body that had a far profounder influence. In the eighteenth century, as we have seen, a high standard of design was set by the cultivated taste of an aristocracy. Though our modern bureaucracy, which acts in the same capacity, has not yet succeeded in acquiring definite enough standards of its own to exert a similar influence, we have had the benefit of some equivalent: namely that of certain big public and industrial corporations, notably the London Transport Board, whose good influence on design in the between-war period was incalculable. Not only were its Underground Stations (see Plate 23) – often placed in instructive contrast in the middle of the worst bogus Tudor housing estates – the most satisfactory series of modern buildings in England, but all the details of their equipment – signs, lettering, staircases, and litter-baskets, and the layout and typography of time-tables – were well thought out and in a consistent modern taste. London Transport posters, moreover, were celebrated all over the world. They employed some of the best living artists and they understood the use of advertisement for decoration as well as for instruction. It is an interesting sign of the influence of poster art that many of the ideas of modern art – cubism, abstract design, surrealism – are employed on posters and liked by the man in the street, when the same things seen in the more serious atmosphere of a picture gallery would be considered outrageous. Which is an indication of the absurd and almost religious

air of respectability with which the academies had surrounded art.

Britain had no individual architects of the calibre of Le
Corbusier or Frank Lloyd Wright, but the number of architects who strove, in the face of much opposition, to establish
modern ideas grew rapidly. In 1931 some of these, together
with other young architects and one or two writers and
scientists, founded the M.A.R.S. Group, whose initials stood
for Modern Architectural Research. Its object was not only
to organize technical and other research, which can be done
collectively so much better than by individuals working on
their own, but also to represent the modern architectural
movement in this country. Up till this date Great Britain
was not represented at all in the C.I.A.M. (Congrès Internationaux d'Architecture Moderne), the parent body of a
number of national groups through which architectural ideas
were being exchanged. In 1938 the M.A.R.S. Group organized an ambitious exhibition of modern architecture at the
New Burlington Galleries in London, which had considerable
influence and which is a landmark so far as the history of
its ideas in this country is concerned.

CHAPTER VII

THE MODERN ARCHITECTURAL
SCENE

THE steady growth of modern architecture, as summarized in the preceding chapters, was brought to an end by the Second World War and the concentration of energy almost everywhere on destructive rather than constructive planning. Between 1939 and 1945, except for spasmodic efforts in neutral Sweden and Switzerland, which were themselves cut off from many essential materials, civilian building flourished only in the South American countries, where an enterprising school of modern architecture had just become established. It had been stimulated by a visit paid by Le Corbusier to Brazil in 1936, and spread afterwards with astonishing rapidity.

Elsewhere the war, happily, meant only a temporary setback, because by now the idea of modern architecture, in Europe and the United States was securely rooted, even if it was not universally accepted and had not reached a very advanced stage of maturity and refinement; so its energies were quickly released again at the end of the war, and leapt the more boldly into action because of the stimulus provided by the vast rebuilding programme that faced a large part of the inhabited world.

With the post-war period our chronological history ceases. We have reached our own generation, and find the architects still engaged in the struggle to translate their enthusiasm for contemporary techniques and ideas into something positive and disciplined: the creation of an improved environment for everyone. The struggle takes different forms in different places. In Soviet Russia it continues to follow the course on which it was already set before the war. Modern science is as fully exploited there as is compatible with the revival of nineteenth-century bourgeois styles and the adaptation of archaic regional traditions. A truly magnificent constructional programme is embodied in cumbersome buildings resembling those from which it was the task of modern architecture to break away, and the obscurantist policy they represent has spread to the other countries within the Soviet orbit: Czechoslovakia, Hungary, Poland, etc. Poland, after her liberation in 1945, showed remarkable energy in rebuilding the utterly devastated city of Warsaw on a new and improved plan, but the architectural ideas that began so promisingly have been transformed, under Soviet influence, into buildings of the same clumsy period-revival character.

It is easy, of course, to condemn this reactionary phase through which Eastern European architecture is passing; just as it is easy for Communist propaganda to condemn the architecture of the West as formalistic. And there is much truth in the latter allegation if it means that Western architecture is too often an architects' not a people's, architecture. For connoisseurship of modern architecture is still largely confined to the professional man and the intelligentsia. This is a defect that time and modern architecture's own ability to cultivate the graces on which popular appreciation rests should succeed in remedying. It is not remedied by looking backwards, or by pandering to the least educated people's fondness for familiar symbols that the changing world has rendered culturally meaningless. People generally, not only architects, can be taught to look forward. Although it is right and natural that people should not blindly support a kind of architecture they feel is remote from them, this should not preclude the creative architects from reaching far ahead of popular taste. That is the way progress is made; the experiment of today is the commonplace of tomorrow. The weakness of the Soviet attitude is that it opens no window on to the future.

It should be added that since about 1958 some of the more elaborately reminiscent characteristics of Soviet architecture have been modified – ostensibly on account of their expense – and several of the other Eastern European countries, especially Poland and Hungary, have largely liberated themselves from Soviet cultural domination and shown in their architecture an appreciation of sophisticated modern ideas closer to that of Western Europe.

Another difference between Eastern and Western Europe is the intense nationalism of the former and its distrust of the international character of much of the modern architecture of the West. This character, however, is specially to be identified with modern architecture's earlier days – so much so that some critics and historians have labelled modern architecture, as it emerged from the experimental period of the nineteen-twenties, the 'international style'. But it has been growing out of this phase ever since before the war. It was clear from the beginning that it was only a temporary one. The new architecture, in that it is a way of approaching architectural problems based on reason instead of on sentiment, is not concerned with frontiers. It grew simultaneously in many different countries, as we have seen, and a modern hospital in Yugoslavia might at first have been interchangeable with one in Belgium, Australia, or California. The kind of civilization that has produced modern architecture, as well as the social needs that provide the occasion for it, is much the same in all countries where it has flourished; but countries also have their own different temperaments and ideals, and different climates, habits, and raw materials. They also have a past, and the national culture of which their modern architecture is part is not separable from its roots, even were that desirable. So, as modern architecture began to mature, a new differentiation according to national characteristics was discernible – not on the basis of the racial exclusiveness of Nazism, and not so clear and distinct as would have been the case many years ago, before steam, the aeroplane, the telephone, and the radio broke down once and for all many national barriers; but Englishness is a definable quality found in things English, as Frenchness is found in things French, and these qualities are not incompatible with modern architecture as we have described it. They are produced as part of our instinctive selection of materials, shapes, and colours; our emotional reaction to climate and to social relations. As mankind is still organized into nations – biologically as well as politically – a permanently international architecture would not be produced even by literal functionalism.

This process of re-nationalization of a common architectural idiom is not in any case a new one. Exactly the same thing happened in the twelfth and thirteenth centuries when the Gothic architecture that was at first common to the whole of Europe began to acquire peculiar characteristics in each country until it culminated in the Perpendicular Gothic of fifteenth-century England, a purely national style. Perhaps the modern equivalent of this kind of development should be described as *regionalism* rather than *nationalism*, to suggest that the geographical boundaries are the important ones, not the political boundaries, and to discriminate against the symbolic nationalism that was fostered by the Fascist countries, and against the sentimental nationalism – the renewed attachment to the traditional forms of the past – that is a source of conflict in many European countries at the time of writing, even those, Holland for example, and to a lesser degree Switzerland, which have long been regarded as the strongholds of modern design. This tendency may be no more than the passing effect of a post-war sense of insecurity, but it shows that the battle for modern architecture is by no means won.

A reaction of a less naive kind has taken place in the Scandinavian countries, especially Sweden, which has alarmed the more doctrinaire exponents of a revolutionary (as distinct from an evolutionary) modern architecture by specializing in a cosy domesticity which appears to turn its back on many of modern architecture's spectacular achievements; not by reviving period styles, but by preferring traditional building techniques and materials and putting the highest value on charm of character and a close accord between building and landscape. But except in the work of Gunnar Asplund, architect of the Stockholm Exhibition of 1930 (Plate 15) and the Stockholm crematorium (Plate 33), Sweden has never contributed much to the revolutionary developments through which modern architecture made its initial impact on the world. She is now only following the tendency already noted as typical of Swedish architecture before the war: to concentrate on good craftsmanship, on spreading good taste widely, and on the preservation of human values, rather than on technical adventure and experiment.

Among the best Swedish achievements are those that closely combine social and architectural developments, such as the carefully planned new towns built in recent years outside Stockholm: Vällingby and Farsta.

In the immediate post-war period, the best place in Europe to see modern architecture at its most vigorous and vital was Italy, where it flourished remarkably. The Italians have always had an instinct for fine building, with a splendid range of materials to exercise it on. They also, like other Mediterranean peoples, have a well developed sense of form, and are therefore content to let a well conceived structure tell its own story. Especially in Rome and Milan, the number of modern buildings of a high average quality is striking; so is the invention and imagination shown in the design of furniture, light fittings, and all kinds of equipment. Since about 1958, however, a reactionary movement, strongest among the younger architects and interior designers, has gained some headway and has somewhat undermined Italy's leading position in the world of modern design. This perverse though well-intentioned movement, known as Neo-Liberty, in searching for a way to develop beyond the doctrinaire formulae of purely rational architecture, has felt it necessary, instead of looking forward, to retreat into reminiscences of *Art Nouveau* and similar past episodes. Another continuing weakness in Italian architecture is the absence of planning; a *laissez faire* attitude to architecture's social responsibilities is evident everywhere, so that in a town with a severe housing shortage it may be found that the only new building is a luxury cinema. But the allocation of priorities is a political as well as an architectural question.

Everywhere in Europe architectural activity since 1945 has been restricted by economic difficulties, but the rebuilding of war-devastated Western Germany has reached an excellent, though sometimes dull, architectural standard, recalling the achievements of that country before the Nazis. Here period styles have practically no place. Not so in France, where Le Corbusier remains a lonely giant in a nation that perhaps, because of his presence, has acquired a higher reputation for architectural enlightenment than it deserves. The average French building shows little awareness that the revolution brought about by modern architecture ever happened. Le Corbusier was given but a small part to play in the reconstruction of war-damaged areas, but completed, in the face of much opposition, one building which, taken all round, is probably the most significant in post-war Europe. This is the *Unité d'Habitation* (Plate 34), a vast apartment block on the outskirts of Marseilles in which he has embodied many of the ideas put forward in his writings. It is a compact, slab-like building, raised on tapering concrete columns, housing 1,600 people in its sixteen storeys and providing them with shopping and other facilities under the same roof. It is described in greater detail in Chapter VIII.

Subsequent works by Le Corbusier have aroused interest just as widespread: his chapel at Ronchamp, a highly personal and imaginative building partaking as much of the quality of sculpture as of architecture, and his monastery at La Tourette in which reinforced concrete is used with unprecedented expressiveness and which shares with Ronchamp a remarkable aesthetic control over the internal use of natural lighting.

To find modern buildings of so adventurous a character in any quantity, we must cross the Atlantic from the old world to the new. The sudden surge of interest in modern architecture in Brazil in the late nineteen-thirties was referred to at the beginning of this chapter. It has since developed in a remarkable way. Under the guidance of Lucio Costa, who in 1936 prompted the Minister of Education to invite Le Corbusier to Brazil to prepare a planning-scheme for the University of Rio de Janeiro, a group of youngish architects has produced a great number of spectacular modern buildings which have changed the face of Rio and São Paulo. Among them are Oscar Niemeyer, who worked with Le Corbusier on his university plan and soon afterwards became the leader of a group which designed the Ministry of Education building at Rio (Plate 21) with Le Corbusier as consulting architect, Rino Levi, Affonso Reidy, and the brothers Marcelo and Milton Roberto.

They are all to some degree disciples of Le Corbusier, and

the imaginative use of pure geometry on which his style is founded has flourished in ideal conditions in the strong South American sunlight, where, too, the functional but at the same time decorative device of the *brise-soleil*, or slatted sun-screen covering the face of a building, which Le Corbusier invented for a block of offices in Algiers in 1933, has found its perfect justification. The new Brazilian architecture has a baroque quality, inherited perhaps from the Portuguese colonial tradition, and an adventurous sense of form to which the quality of its finish is not always equal. An appropriate regional flavour is given by the revival, for decorative use outside as well as in, of the Latin-American tradition of the *azuleijo* or painted ceramic title.

In recent years additional attention has been focused on Brazil because of one spectacular experiment taking place there: the building of a brand new capital city – Brasilia – in the uninhabited interior highlands of the country. The plan is by Lucio Costa and many of the principal buildings are by Niemeyer. The first of these to be finished, the President's palace (see Plate 41) and the Parliament buildings, carried yet another stage further the combination of imaginative form and technical sophistication for which Brazil was already noted.

Architecture has also made great strides forward in other South American countries (notably Venezuela) and in Mexico, where a new university city constitutes one of the largest groups of modern buildings in the world, and since 1954 Japan has joined vigorously in the movement. But the main centre of activity in the years since 1945 has undoubtedly been the United States. Here, as explained in the last chapter, modern architecture was at first regarded simply as a new style imported from Europe, to be put on a level with the revived historical styles, and was not associated with Louis Sullivan's pioneering achievements in Chicago or with the demands that Frank Lloyd Wright had been making for years for an architecture that should rise naturally from the conditions of site and structure and express profounder ideals than those of fashion and prestige.

But gradually, and helped first by the activities of the Museum of Modern Art in New York, which put on exhibitions of the new architecture of Europe, and then by the arrival of some of the leading architects of Europe as refugees, including Walter Gropius, Marcel Breuer, Mies van der Rohe, Moholy-Nagy, and Jose Luis Sert, who had years of struggle on behalf of modern architecture behind them, its principles became better understood. Its practicality and efficiency were recognized and it was seen, too, to respond to the special American urge to enjoy to the full the advantages modern science has to offer. Although prestige building, using reminiscences of period styles, is still not unknown, and there is much flashy design that deserves the description modernistic rather than modern, a modern approach to the design of buildings is now taken for granted in America, as in few other countries, and is reflected in the teaching at most of the architectural schools.

Modern American architecture is, however, by no means standardized in style. The many regions and climates of which the United States is composed, and the presence of influential personalities in certain centres, have combined to produce a number of distinct schools of design. For example the New England school of domestic architecture, employed by Gropius and Breuer and aiming at a modern equivalent of the white-boarded farmhouse, with its fieldstone fireplaces, of the Atlantic seaboard, can be contrasted with the California school, of which Richard Neutra is the chief exponent. Here the sub-tropical climate dictates widely spreading eaves and a merging of airy indoor rooms with outdoor garden terraces and shady patios, following a tradition established by earlier Californian architects like Green and Maybeck. Houses of this kind have, of course, much in common with the famous Prairie houses of Frank Lloyd Wright.

The significance of Wright's work has been discussed in an earlier chapter and the small recognition at first given to it in his own country noted. But in the nineteen-forties a new interest in his ideas developed, and the study of his buildings was another factor that helped forward the understanding of modern architecture. Finally he became a nationally revered figure. One of his last important buildings, a research laboratory at Racine, Wisconsin, a tower with the floors cantilevered from a central stair and lift-shaft, sheathed externally in glass, showed that he had lost none of his imaginative power or freshness of outlook.

When Wright died in 1959 he had just completed a more controversial building – the Guggenheim Museum in New York City in the form of a continuous spiral ramp on the walls of which the pictures are hung, which was criticized as being impractical and for its clumsy finish. But it, too, exemplified his special attitude to planning that he termed organic; that is, planning that allows the outward form of the building to emerge naturally from the way it is to be used.

Another contrast is afforded by the sophisticated urban style identified with the German architect Mies van der Rohe, who has been settled in Chicago since 1937 and has completed several buildings for the Illinois Institute of Technology (Plate 39) and a striking series of apartment blocks on Lake Shore Drive, Chicago. These are masterpieces of precise engineering, devoid of any ornament, or of qualities (such as those arising from the effects of the weather or from the varying textures of natural materials) that cannot be exactly controlled. They rely for their aesthetic effect on subtlety of proportion and mechanical precision of finish. Mies van der

Rohe has acquired an enthusiastic following, some of whom, notably Philip Johnson, have shown in their own work that the seemingly puritanical attitude of mind that makes a virtue of the industrialization of building methods can transform the cold mechanical rhythms which arise from these methods into a quite magical feeling for the interplay of enclosed and semi-enclosed space.

Mies van der Rohe and Philip Johnson collaborated on a recent New York skyscraper, the Seagram Building, which is the last word in such buildings in the sense that it makes of it a finite monument that it is difficult to see being developed any further.

Mies van der Rohe was until recently also director of the Architectural Department at Illinois Institute of Technology. The presence of eminent European architects teaching and practising where they teach has done much, in other places besides Chicago, to spread modern ideas among the younger American architects. Gropius, as well as being, until 1952, Professor of Architecture at Harvard, designed, in conjunction with a group of his ex-students, calling themselves the Architects' Collaborative, a significant building – the new Graduate Centre – for Harvard University, as well as several others; and Alvar Aalto, the Finnish architect, who taught for a while at the Massachusetts Institute of Technology in the nineteen-forties, designed a vigorous dormitory building there.

But let it not be thought that all America's architectural professors are recent arrivals from Europe. Successive heads of the Architectural Department at M.I.T. have been W. W. Wurster, a San Francisco architect noted in the nineteen-thirties for his informally planned timber houses, and Pietro Belluschi, an architect of Italian extraction whose office buildings in Portland, Oregon, and elsewhere, built during the first years after the war, showed a cleanness of line and slick simplicity of rhythm that have now become the hallmarks of American commercial architecture; and the late director of the architectural department at Yale University – another influential school – was George Howe, former partner of Lescaze, whose Philadelphia skyscraper (Plate 20) has already been referred to as one of the best of its day.

Other American architects, besides those already mentioned, whose work has been outstanding in various fields (omitting designers of private houses, the good specimens of which are too numerous to mention) are Eero Saarinen (son of the Finnish architect Eliel Saarinen, with whom he designed a number of educational buildings in Michigan and Illinois), Charles Eames (who has also made his mark as a pioneer furniture designer), Harrison and Abramovitz (designers of the Alcoa Building, an aluminium-sheathed skyscraper in Pittsburgh), Ernest Kump and Co. (designers of schools in the San Francisco region), Louis Kahn (whose recent medical research building for Pennsylvania University has aroused world-wide interest), Bruce Goff, Hugh Stubbins, Minoru Yamasaki (an American of Japanese origin who has specialized in decorative wall treatments derived from precast concrete and other industrially produced elements), Ralph Rapson, John Johansen, I. M. Pei, Paul Rudolph and – perhaps the firm of architects most characteristic of progressive American tendencies – Skidmore, Owings, and Merrill, who have shown how, by good organization, quantity production of architectural designs in places wide apart can remain compatible with real creative ability. The chief designer of S.O.M. (as this huge firm with offices all over America is generally called) is Gordon Bunshaft.

America, unlike Germany, Holland, and the Scandinavian countries (and, in recent years, Britain), has never paid much attention to the architectural problems posed by, and the opportunities offered by, low-rent public-authority housing.

But a few enterprising projects, like those in the south-west, by Cairns and De Mars, for the Farm Security Administration, and some of those initiated by the Government as emergency wartime measures, have awakened interest in the subject and a quantity of well-planned public housing is now being carried out. It is a branch of architecture that presents a strong challenge to the American genius for large-scale organization and her ability to develop new techniques based on industrialization – techniques of the kind that European architects have assiduously studied without possessing the industrial resources to exploit them.

Industry and commerce are the natural outlets for America's architectural energies, and the former has made marked progress since the hey-day of the vast architectural offices, which combined engineering achievement with a somewhat clumsy striving after architectural effect. In Eero Saarinen's General Motors Factory at Detroit, engineering and architecture are fused into an expressive whole. Commercial architecture, in other countries besides America, has helped to familiarize the public with the outward forms favoured by modern architecture by exploiting them for display purposes; in this lies a danger of too much value being given to novelty. Novelty is not an architectural quality, and commerce, in the pursuit of novelty, is apt not to discriminate between the genuine and the false; so architecture, though it owes a debt to commerce for its spirit of enterprise, also owes to commerce the worst examples of 'modernistic' design.

Many American shops and stores, nevertheless, are good examples of modern design, and new types of building, like the out-of-town shopping centre built close to a main highway, an expression of the complete assimilation of the motor-car into American life, have fostered a spirit of experiment. There is one outside Los Angeles, by Gruen and

Krummeck, which is particularly exciting visually. Most people, however, identify American commercial architecture with the high city office-block. We have already observed some of the stages this peculiarly American phenomenon has passed through. In keeping with the general trend of American architecture, the best recent examples fuse architecture and structure more completely and more satisfactorily than any comparable buildings since those of W. L. Jenney and Louis Sullivan in the 1880s. The United Nations Secretariat, beside New York's East River, designed by an international team of architects (of whom Le Corbusier was an active member) led by Wallace K. Harrison, is typical of the almost diagrammatic type of building that the skyscraper has lately become: a flat slab, its sides faced with glass, its ends with marble, getting its aesthetic effect solely from the scale and rhythm of its structural frame and glass infilling.

An even better example is the Lever Building, New York (Plate 40), by Skidmore, Owings, and Merrill, showing the use of frame construction to raise the whole building on columns, allowing the ground to flow beneath it. It may be regarded as typical of that school of modern architecture which exploits the drama of technical perfection.

We must now turn our attention to Britain, which has been left to the last as the country that chiefly concerns readers of this book. In the preceding chapter we left her, at the outbreak of war in 1939, with modern architectural ideas well established but making slow headway against conservatism and official timidity. Britain's experience since the war has been a mixture of disappointment and fulfilment.

The war ended with a desperate need for buildings of all kinds and a new generation of architects eager to respond to it. The disappointment arises from the fact that national economic circumstances – the necessity to restrict capital expenditure on building – limited the building programme to a fraction of what was needed. The architect's scope was thereby restricted in two ways: the Government was compelled to forbid, as a general rule, all building except the three most essential kinds – housing, schools, and factories – and so much emphasis was – and still is – placed on cheapness as altogether to inhibit the architect's free exercise of his art.

There was a time (for example immediately after 1918) when the need for economy was to be welcomed as imposing a healthy discipline on the architect, compelling him to cut out the frills and concentrate on essentials; but the degree of austerity now demanded of him leaves too little scope for the play of imagination and too little opportunity to extend the range of modern architecture's vocabulary by the use of high-quality finish and beautiful materials. It is a bad thing that a whole generation of architects is growing up that has had no experience of using luxurious materials. Doing the job more cheaply than the next man is too often the architect's principal means of earning credit with his client, and English architecture will be the poorer for this for a long time to come.

But there is a more cheerful side to economic stringency. The strict allocation of what capital could be spared for building for the most essential purposes – housing, schools, and factories – meant that architecture was brought into close relationship with social needs as never before. Architects were given a chance to study the social responsibilities of their profession and work in close collaboration with housing managers, education officers, and the other local government officials in whose hands a large part of the nation's building programme had been placed.

And they had town-planning legislation aimed at ensuring that the right buildings went up in the right places. As a result of the Town and Country Planning Act passed in 1947, Britain's town-planning laws are as enlightened as any in the

115

world. Some of the provisions of this complex measure, such as those that deal with compensation to landowners and with vesting in the State any increased value that land acquires because of the new developments taking place on or near it, proved cumbersome in application and have already been revised; but its general effect is to enable the siting of all buildings, and the use to which all land is put, to be controlled and planned in advance in the public interest. Although the usefulness of this, like other legislation, depends in practice on the intelligence of the men who operate it (in this instance on the County Planning Officers), the Town and Country Planning Act should succeed in preventing a repetition of those mistakes, such as ribbon-building along main roads and the scattering of unplanned housing estates over precious agricultural country, which marred the broad picture of British architecture before the war.

But we are concerned here with building more than with planning. It was realized before the end of the war that Britain's most urgent building need would be some millions of new houses, and that the only means of producing them quickly enough was to treat the whole problem as an industrial operation, mass-producing standard parts of houses in factories for rapid assembly on the site. This was an idea wholly in keeping with the principles of modern architecture; indeed it represented but a further step in the direction in which it had been slowly travelling since the Industrial Revolution, and the architects were ready to take it. Some promising designs for prefabricated houses were made, but the plans for using them were thrown out of gear by successive shortages of the two materials first employed – timber and steel – and by the excessive cost of a third material tried – aluminium; and the plans eventually broke down altogether because no real effort was made to put into effect the reorganization of the building industry that was required for a nationally planned undertaking of this kind. The industry was still organized on an individualistic, handicraft basis, and remains largely so today. Although a number of pre-fabricated houses were constructed, including bungalows for erection on temporarily vacant sites to help tide over the emergency, the housing programme as a whole gradually reverted to traditional methods, and now the great majority of new houses are being laboriously built in the old way, using brick walls and tiled roofs.

It was a failure of political and industrial planning rather than of architecture, though if it had succeeded the effect on architecture would have been immeasurably beneficial. For the time being we must be content with the lesser benefits – better planning, a simpler and more discreet appearance, more intelligent grouping – that the post-war housing drive undoubtedly brought with it. There is still much badly designed housing, often the work of builders and surveyors rather than architects, but in spite of the restrictions imposed by old-fashioned methods of building, the control exercised by local authorities and their architects has brought about a most welcome change since the speculative builder dominated the scene before the war. This control can probably be seen at its best in some of the new towns that are being built round London to take some of its excess population. Harlow (architect-planner, Frederick Gibberd) is probably the best of these architecturally, but on the whole the new towns are disappointingly un-town-like in their layout, retaining the spread-out character of the pre-war housing estate.

To see what modern architecture (in the special sense in which we are using the term) can do for housing we must go to the big cities, especially London, where shortage of space compels housing to take the form of high blocks of flats. The architects of these, though severely restricted as to cost, have been given many opportunities to experiment, and some first-rate buildings have resulted. Among the best schemes are one by Armstrong and MacManus in Chelsea, another by the same architects in St Pancras, with flats and maisonettes grouped round a sequence of squares and thus following (but in a completely modern style) the pattern on the ground that had existed there since the early nineteenth century, one on the northern edge of the City, at Golden Lane, by Chamberlin, Powell and Bon, and, most striking of all, a large riverside scheme in Pimlico (see Plate 43) by Powell and Moya.

All these are working-class flats designed by private architects for local authorities. Many of the latter have their own architectural offices. Not all are very progressive in their ideas, but an important exception is the London County Council, notable for its willingness to experiment and for the high quality of its designs. The L.C.C. is responsible for several large housing schemes of exceptional quality in the Wimbledon–Roehampton areas, in which tall blocks of flats stand up among terraces of houses and maisonettes, imaginatively disposed among the trees in what once were the gardens of large Victorian houses. The L.C.C. is being superseded (1965) by the Greater London Council, covering an ever wider area, and there is every hope that its high standards will be maintained. Outside London, more belatedly, excellent schemes of a similar kind have been built by the city architects of several cities – notably Sheffield.

The enterprise and leadership shown by some local authorities are among the most encouraging things about post-war architecture in Britain. They are seen to special advantage in school building. In the years after the war, the Hertfordshire County Council produced a series of schools that were among the most advanced, and aesthetically the most attractive, of any contemporary buildings in Britain. Faced with the need to build a large number of schools quickly, the Hertfordshire County Architect, C. H. Aslin, and his deputy, S. Johnson-Marshall, devised, with the help of a manufacturer, a constructional system based on a light framework and consisting of standard structural and walling units which could be produced in large quantities and delivered to the site ready for use. This was the first attempt on a large scale to apply industrial methods to the technique of building, and resulted not only in speed and economy but in efficiently planned buildings with a delightfully fresh and airy character. More details are given in the notes to Plate 42.

Other local-authority architects have experimented successfully in a similar direction, and a number of private architects, employed by county education authorities, have designed school buildings embodying the same qualities of flexible planning, good lighting, and a graceful appearance. Among them are the partnership of Yorke, Rosenberg, and Mardall, and Denis Clarke-Hall, whose pre-war school at Richmond, Yorkshire, was the first example of modern school architecture in England.

There is no space to do more than name some of the other British architects who – in addition to those already mentioned on pages 85 and 118 or elsewhere in this book – have set the high standard by which modern British architecture and town design can now claim to be judged: Denys Lasdun, Gollins, Melvin and Ward, Farmer and Dark, Eric Lyons, Donald Gibson (until 1955 City Architect of Coventry), Ernö Goldfinger, W. G. Holford, Robert Matthew, J. L. Martin (the two latter both at different times architect to the London County Council), Richard Llewelyn Davies, Richard Sheppard, Basil Spence, and the group known as the Architects' Co-Partnership. The influence of the engineers, like Ove Arup and the late F. J. Samuely, who have worked closely with modern architects, should also not be ignored; nor that of writers like John Summerson, Nikolaus Pevsner, and Robert Furneaux Jordan.

Six years after the war British architects were allowed their first brief holiday from the utilitarian tasks to which they were otherwise wholly confined. The South Bank Exhibition of the 1951 Festival occupied a splendid riverside site in the centre of London. The thirty or so architects engaged on it, led by Sir Hugh Casson, took full advantage of the opportunity to exercise their fancy and to indulge in the kind of experiments, technical and aesthetic, that it has always been the role of exhibition architecture, because of its temporary nature, to encourage. The result (Plate 44), lively and colourful, provided a tonic that English architecture badly needed, and proved to the public, who had hitherto seen modern architecture only in a more or less utilitarian guise, that it was also capable of richness and fantasy.

One permament building formed part of the exhibition layout: the Royal Festival Hall (Plate 45), a concert hall designed to be the first instalment of a new cultural centre planned for this vacant Thames-side site. The first major public building put up in England after the war, with its foyer-space flowing between the pillars on which the great auditorium is raised up, and its glimpses through screens of glass of one interior space leading on to another and one level giving way to another, it is a brave attempt to create the dignity and impressiveness that a public building ought to have out of those effects – the play of space, the drama of frankly revealed construction, the enjoyment of finely finished materials – which the modern architect regards as specially his own.

Here is one more instance of a public authority giving modern architecture its chance, but it should not be thought, because of this and the other examples of enlightened patronage mentioned above, that the battle for modern architecture in Britain is anything like over. A walk down any city street that has been the scene of recent building activity will show how far we still have to progress. If the street contains a new bank or office building it may still boast an elaborate façade with the full panoply of classical columns and entablature, similar to most buildings of fifty or even a hundred years ago, but even less justifiable on account of the hidden steel skeleton whose structural nature the ornamental stonework belies. Next door there may be a more up-to-date block of offices or flats without period ornament, which has been omitted in the interests of fashion, but still harking back to a different period when the available sizes of stone lintels dictated the width of window openings. Nearby there may be one of those striking buildings that have adopted and exaggerated the superficial lines of modern architecture as a new form of decoration which is best described as jazz-modern. This one could not have existed without modern architecture as its inspiration, but it has very little more to do with it than the Renaissance bank or the neo-classical office block. It is probably a super cinema. Thus does the variegated architecture of a single street jump arbitrarily from one century to another and from one assumed costume to another. Inside, these buildings may be full of the raw material of modern architecture. The example of the beautiful mechanism of the bank's steel strong-room doors is alone enough to inspire an ambition to carry the same quality of purposeful and refined craftsmanship into architecture itself. The complexities of planning and organization that were needed to house satisfactorily such an elaborate machine as, say, a department store or a newspaper office deserved more recognition and more appropriate expression than the conventional 'architected' façades that this street consists of: sometimes merely academic, more often nowadays in some whimsical or fashionable 'taste'.

However, this is a familiar story. But as I have tried to show in this book, there is now a modern architecture that has progressed a good deal beyond the inspiration offered by the raw material of modern life. The pooled experience of many years is now available for our benefit. In this country itself we can now study and criticize examples of what a sensible modern architecture might be like.

But it is the misfortune of architecture that it needs more than a school of progressive architects to produce a general condition of good building. The architect cannot, like the painter or musician in the seclusion of his studio, labour at the production of masterpieces and present the finished product to the world whether the world welcomes it or no, leaving perhaps distant posterity to appreciate its worth. The architect is tied to his patron. Each of his works is the fulfilment of a particular programme, not set, as with the artist, by the reaction of his own sensibilities to the circumstances that surround him or by the vision he himself creates, but set by the practical needs and wishes of someone else. Only the quality of the work as art depends on his own vision.

Further, the 'someone else' whose word of command the architect's talent awaits transforms itself for the purpose of patronage into a sum of money. Architectural design, economically speaking, equals capital invested in property. So the architect is tied to whoever puts up the money for building schemes and is often handicapped by the rather illogical working of our business system.

A most encouraging symptom of the present time is the spread of patronage from the enlightened individual to the public body. Yet until it spreads far more widely the present waste, resulting from the architect's specialized knowledge not being made full use of, will continue. Whenever a building is put up according to out-of-date methods whose failings have already been demonstrated elsewhere – a block of flats planned round enclosed courts so that the noise of children playing is magnified by reverberation round the walls; a town-hall council chamber built the wrong shape for good hearing; the windows of a school of the wrong kind to preserve the scholar's eyesight; or even the larder in a house with a window facing south – that is evidence of the most expert advice not sought or not taken. These are strictly practical points, but it is not unreasonable for the architects of the kind we have labelled 'modern' to boast that it is they who take points such as these most closely into consideration, partly because of their scientific outlook and habit of thoroughly analysing needs before beginning to design, and partly of course because if a building is designed pictorially, simply as a number of façades or as a picturesque shape, some of the requirements of architectural 'composition' are bound to conflict with the requirements of the building's interior.

This is largely a question of competence, not of modernity, but the fact remains that people are learning to appreciate modern architecture through its practical advantages; that modernism has entered the home, as it were through the kitchen. Moreover, as I have already pointed out, the practical side of modern architecture is not really separable from the aesthetic; a fact which gives it much of its vitality. So when we look at modern architecture as it flourishes in England today, and find that some types of building show a remarkable awareness of its charms and possibilities while others seem almost blind to its existence, we cannot explain it by saying that taste in styles of architecture varies. Much more than taste is at stake: sheer efficiency, as well as imagination, purpose, vision, are all directed against falsity in architecture and against the sentimentality that prefers an inconvenient, extravagant, old-fashioned – even obviously ugly – building to one whose appearance is the least bit unfamiliar, and which lacks the comforting associations that the traditional styles possess.

Nevertheless modern architecture is not a thing that can be adopted as an enlightened business man might adopt a new system of cash-accounting, and, possibly, discard it when it is no longer fashionable. Good modern architecture is the result of a new way of thinking about what buildings are for and an open mind about what they are going to look like.

Patrons of different kinds may come and go, but the future of architecture lies eventually in what kind of buildings people demand. Rather than make an effort to admire a strange thing called 'modern architecture' because it is theoretically on the right lines, one would prefer that people simply asked themselves exactly what they want from architecture. When once they have succeeded in eliminating their prejudices and habits about architecture – wanting columns, for example, not for architectural reasons but because they have the habit of associating columns with luxury and pomp, or wanting Tudor gables on their houses because of the cosiness they associate with 'Olde Worlde' styles, they will realize that architecture, which is the whole setting of their lives, could do a great deal more for them than it does. What they want is well planned cities composed of buildings that are also well planned because the real needs of the inhabitants have been studied; buildings, moreover, that make full use of what modern science can provide, and, finally, use it with art and imagination so that the buildings are themselves a pleasure and an inspiration. This programme suggests something quite different from the conventional architecture of our time. It is the programme which the architecture we have been calling modern is struggling to fulfil.

To conclude this chapter something should be said about modern buildings in relation to old buildings, and their effect on the English countryside. It is often said that the great open spaces of America or Russia may be suitable for a new architecture, but that in this country, with our intensive use of space of which every square yard is part of our own history, innovation should be looked at differently. Our landscape is not wild nature but is a man-made setting for a well-established way of living. We are proud of our architectural heritage, and sometimes feel that the brand-new forms of a machine-age architecture are an affront to the mellowness of our tradition. It is even said that whatever the merits of modern buildings, one does not want to see them in the middle of Oxford or Cambridge or in a cathedral city.

This attitude indicates a complete misunderstanding of the way architecture evolves. Before last century every building was modern when it was new. It is only recently that modern building has had to compete with imitation old building. The English scene having shown itself capable of assimilating any number of quite revolutionary changes, there is no reason why it should not equally assimilate whatever innovations today is bringing to it. The typical English landscape as we know it is entirely the creation of the late eighteenth century, when the design of the whole view was first regarded as an art. In the nineteenth century the railway was regarded as a threat to the very existence of rural peace and beauty, but so well has it been absorbed that the perspective of railway lines, the geometry of cutting and embankment, and the plume of smoke travelling across the middle distance are now typical features in an English pastoral landscape. In our turn we can absorb the arterial road and the electric pylon, and make something equally full of character out of them. After all, the conventional outlook of resenting whatever disturbs the repose of nature would logically find the highest degree of vandalism in the distant view of the ordinary village church spire.

Architecture has in some periods taken pains to acquire,

as it were, the protective colouring of its own background; at other times it has taken a pride in shining out as the focal point in a carefully designed landscape. The Cotswold stone cottage is an example of the first: the Regency stucco mansion standing in a Suffolk park an example of the second. Each is a precedent that in suitable circumstances our own day can follow. The only fatal attitude is to treat the countryside as a museum exhibit to be preserved rather than developed. If it is not used for whatever demands modern life may make on it, its character, based as it is on a tradition of use, will lose all meaning. It may be added that the one thing that has done more in recent times than anything else to ruin the country-side, the unplanned small-house development on the outskirts of our cities and along the coastline, is the one that ignores the principles behind modern architecture most completely. From the point of view of land utilization alone the planning of new housing in an orderly systematic way according to up-to-date principles would have saved acres of country from being ruined; and this apart from the fact that such housing would have provided better places to live in.

Our unwillingness to face the test of putting modern buildings alongside the finest old buildings is presumably due to mistrust of our own architects' ability to keep to the standard set by their predecessors. But surely our best chance of maintaining a high standard of building lies in going about it in the way that is most natural for us. To imitate antique styles because we are building in a University town or Cathedral city is an insult to the very architecture we hold in such respect. There are places, of course, that form a perfect whole in themselves, that we would be sorry to disturb, particularly where the value of the architecture depends on the broad treatment of a large area: the Georgian squares of Bloomsbury, for example, the front at Brighton, the Cathedral Close at Salisbury, and the major portion of Cheltenham, Leamington, and Bath. These are legitimate cases for preservation. If they can reasonably be made to serve modern purposes they should be left to do so intact. For a belief in the possibilities of modern architecture is not incompatible with admiration for the old: indeed the two amount to the same thing, for the qualities of good architecture are unchanging. But where necessity demands that we rebuild, as well as where new needs mean building in new places, to have the courage of our own convictions, allowing us to build frankly for our own time, is the only true way of maintaining the traditions we have inherited.

CHAPTER VIII

SOME MODERN BUILDINGS

THE following pages contain some notes on the buildings shown in the illustrations, written with the purpose of explaining more clearly, with the aid of examples, the various points about modern architecture that have been discussed on the previous pages. The first group of illustrations is concerned with the history and early development of modern architecture. They illustrate Chapter V, where this history is outlined, and represent the various places, personalities, and movements in which the seeds of modern architecture germinated. The other illustrations show modern architecture itself, as put into practice on the Continent of Europe, in America, and in England. If a disproportionate number of the illustrations seems to have been given to England, in spite of the fact that modern architecture has been established longer on the Continent, this is partly because English buildings mean more to us, as they serve needs we are familiar with, and partly because the English examples are more accessible for readers to look at. It is important to do this whenever possible, as a photograph is a poor substitute for a building in the flesh.

It is indeed one of the difficulties that modern architecture has to cope with in making itself widely understood, that so few people have actually seen and explored a modern building. They get their ideas about them from the pseudo-modern and from illustrations. They cannot be expected to appreciate modern buildings until they have really studied them.

In many cases the notes are accompanied by a plan, for the plan is often of great importance in explaining the structural form the building takes. Planning is so much the basis of all architectural design that is recommended that the arrangement of the plan be kept in mind when each photograph is being studied.

The illustrations of modern English buildings have been selected both as representing a wide and typical variety of architectural types, and as representing some of the best work that has been done in this country since modern ideas were introduced. For naturally in modern architecture as well as in so-called traditional (or 'period revival') architecture there are people who are better at it than others, whether because they have more experience or simply because they have more talent of the kind architectural design demands. The not-so-good academic architects are apt to produce uglier buildings than the not-so-good modern architects, because the latter's buildings are at least simple and the former's are generally aggressively complicated. On the other hand, because there are no historical details to remember, no correct sequence of mouldings to get right, and so on, it might appear that there was less skill in the design of a modern building. But as a matter of fact for this very reason to be a good modern architect is at the present moment far more difficult. He is thrown so much more on his own resources. He has to work out everything himself instead of being able to fall back on formulae worked out by other people. This is why the question I have already discussed, of the formation of an accepted modern architectural language, is so important. The special sense in which modern architecture is still largely experimental is this: good modern architecture is only being produced by outstanding architects. But before we can reach an *age* of good architecture we must be in a state where decent modern architecture can be produced by decent ordinary architects – the rank and file of the profession, men that form the backbone of any profession, who know their job but are not geniuses.

The production of a few fine buildings is really no criterion of architecture generally, *vide* the nineteenth century, when architecture as a whole was at a low ebb, although a number of remarkably good buildings were produced by talented individuals: King's Cross Station, St George's Hall Liverpool, Euston Great Arch, Alexander Thompson's churches in Glasgow, and the Houses of Parliament. It is because of its universal standard of good, and at the same time orderly, design that we look back on the eighteenth century as a golden age.

In a few years' time many of the buildings that we regard as being important and remarkable contributions to modern architecture, some of which are illustrated here, may not be regarded as remarkable at all – except to historians of the development of modern architecture. They will look dull and rather tentative attempts to do, with over-much consciousness, what architects of the future will be doing as a matter of course. They are the experiments of individuals; they are still only part of the process of working out a contemporary architectural language.

The photographs on the illustration pages are divided into three groups: first, landmarks in the history and early development of modern architecture during the nineteenth century and the first years of the twentieth, illustrating Chapter V; second, pioneer modern buildings of the period between the two world wars, illustrating Chapter VI; third, some representative modern buildings. More detailed descriptions of the buildings illustrated, and plans of some of them, are given in the remainder of this chapter.

THE BEGINNINGS OF MODERN ARCHITECTURE
Plates 1 to 10 illustrate the early history of modern architecture as outlined in Chapter V. In them one can see the ideas on which modern architecture itself is based first showing themselves. They span the century preceding the war of 1914–

1918. The fine range of warehouses forming part of St Katharine's Docks, just down-river from the Tower of London, is typical of the work of the early nineteenth-century engineers, of which Thomas Telford was probably the greatest. In this work Telford collaborated with the architect Hardwick. Their straightforward use of materials, in this case the yellow stock bricks made from London clay, is combined with a

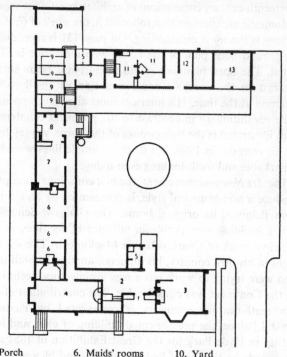

1. Porch
2. Hall
3. Living-room
4. Dining-room
5. Cloak-room
6. Maids' rooms
7. Kitchen
8. Scullery
9. Store-rooms and larders
10. Yard
11. Manservant's living-room and kitchen
12. Stable
13. Coach-house

GROUND FLOOR PLAN OF A HOUSE AT NORTH LUFFENHAM, RUTLAND, by C. F. A. Voysey. *See Plate 3.*

feeling for scale and proportion that belongs to architecture rather than to mere engineering. It is not surprising that works of this kind, achieving such noble effects by such simple means, should now be considered the real architecture of the early nineteenth century. Red House, at Bexley Heath, is unique. William Morris built it, and it stands for the first attempts to escape back to sanity from the artificiality of mid-nineteenth-century conceptions of architecture. Of the school of domestic architecture that followed it, the work of C. F. A. Voysey is the most outstanding. On page 131 is reproduced the ground floor plan of the house whose exterior is illustrated. The open planning round a courtyard bears strong contrast to the compact conglomeration of small rooms common at the time. His interiors must also have appeared quite revolutionary in contrast to the prevalent ornateness. That illustrated is the living-room of the house Voysey built for his own use in 1899, but its clean simple lines would be remarkable and fresh-looking even today.

The *Art Nouveau* movement, the first conscious attempt to produce a non-historical style, is represented by an interior from Belgium, its original home. The Glasgow School of Art, a building remarkably in advance of its time, is the principal work of Charles Rennie Mackintosh. Though but slight in his own country, his influence among the architects who were trying to work out a new architectural technique on the Continent was considerable. The contribution of the nineteenth-century engineers is represented by Paxton's Crystal Palace, the prefabricated building of glass and iron put up in Hyde Park for the Great Exhibition of 1851 and afterwards on the top of Sydenham Hill, and by a vast hall constructed of steel for the Paris Exhibition of 1889, the same exhibition for which Eiffel built his steel tower. Next is one of Louis Sullivan's forthright business buildings in Chicago, where for the first time the steel frame produced its own expressive style of architecture. Typical houses are illustrated by Adolph Loos and Frank Lloyd Wright, pioneers of a new architecture in Austria and America – see Chapter V. Peter Behrens's Turbine factory in Berlin has been called the first real modern building. The steel roof is frankly allowed to dictate the outline of the building, and the flank wall consists of exposed steel stanchions framing huge windows. It is simple, yet rich in character. So subtly are the huge masses of walling composed that its size is only apparent when we notice the smallness of the figures in the foreground. Finally, the French experiments in the use of reinforced concrete are exemplified by the airship hangars at Orly in which a famous engineer first showed what structural beauty this new material lent itself to.

PIONEER WORK BETWEEN THE WARS IN EUROPE, AMERICA, AND BRITAIN

PLATE 11. The top photograph shows the *Bauhaus* at Dessau, Walter Gropius's famous university of design (see Chapter VI). The big block on the right contains the workshops, and a bridge over the road connects it with the library and classrooms. The buildings are of steel and concrete. The large areas of glass that let floods of light into the workshops and laboratories would only be possible in a type of construction that does away with weight-bearing walls. The walls are merely curtains between the floors, which are themselves supported outwards from columns inside the building. The quality that gives life to an otherwise severe design is the subtle rhythm and relationship between the various rectangular units of which the wall-surfaces are made up. The bottom photograph shows that portion of the Siemensstadt housing scheme near Berlin that Gropius himself designed, one of the many great *Siedlungen* round the outskirts of Berlin. Portions of the Siemensstadt *Siedlung* were designed by different architects, with Walter Gropius directing the whole scheme. The picture shows the spacious planning of the great block of flats, with ample space left for gardens and playgrounds. The only possible way of planning a new residential quarter satisfactorily is to do it on a big enough scale to allow a generous layout of this sort and to justify economically the provision of schools, shopping centres, and community buildings in convenient relationship with the flats or houses themselves. Moreover, the modern development of motor traffic makes it essential to re-plan as well as rebuild on a big scale so as to get away from the dangerous and quite unnecessary convention of building in strips alongside the streets.

Modern architects have not concentrated on flats as a type of housing. Small houses are often more suitable, particularly where children need easy access to the garden. The row of working-class houses by a Dutch architect (lower picture, Plate 12) shares with the Berlin flats the merit of having been planned on a large enough scale to allow the row to be designed as a whole. Contrast this with much suburban English housing, where individual plots contain a series of unrelated villas, each competing for attention with its neighbour. Not only is this way of doing it far neater and more dignified, but compact planning in terrace formation – a thing we in England did better than anyone up to about 100 years ago – leaves most space free for gardens and open spaces; or, alternatively, accommodates more people on a given space without having to crowd them into high flats.

PLATE 12 (top): modern structural principles applied to the purposes of transport. Robert Maillart, a Swiss engineer, built a series of magnificent bridges in which the possibilities of reinforced concrete for this sort of purpose were most imaginatively exploited. The bridge illustrated is typical, and shows the litheness and grace obtainable with reinforced concrete construction, to be contrasted with the more massive effect that comes from the use of solid masonry. Though Maillart's bridges may only strike us as possessing the natural grace of efficient engineering structures, when he designed them between 1905 and 1935 he had to face unrelenting persecution and criticism on account of their unorthodoxy.

PLATE 13. The pioneer of the application of reinforced concrete to strictly architectural purposes, as distinct from engineering purposes like bridges, was the Frenchman Auguste Perret (see page 77). This church near Paris derives its whole character from the use of forms natural to this material: slender pillars, segmental vaults, windows in the form of geometrical grilles. It is interesting that the result is so gothic in feeling; both Perret's concrete churches and medieval gothic churches glory in exhibiting the bare bones of their structure. In his other work Perret combined his understanding of new materials with a love of the architectural discipline that goes with the French classical tradition.

PLATE 14. Le Corbusier has perhaps moved further than anyone else away from the idea of a building as consisting of several rigidly defined floors and four solid façades. He saw in modern constructional technique the opportunity it offered of inventing quite free geometrical compositions in which the enclosure of space in various ways might be said to be the method of design, instead of the arrangement of walls. The first floor plan, reproduced on page 136, of the house in the top picture, shows how the possibility of concentrating the loads that have to be carried on a few columns or short lengths of walling allows complete freedom in planning both for convenience and effect. A striking change has taken place since the Voysey house, previously illustrated, which was itself remarkable for being so informally arranged, but only within the limitations imposed by solid masonry construction.

The picture of the house at Garches is taken from the garden and shows the first floor terrace, partly open and partly covered, with steps leading down from it. On this floor all the principal rooms are arranged, the ground floor being given up to a garage, store-rooms, and a small entrance hall from which stairs rise to the proper entrance hall at first-floor level. As can be seen on the plan, the ground floor entrance hall rises two floors in height, and the living-room is open to it along one side, forming a kind of balcony. On the floor above are three bedrooms and two more sitting-rooms.

The interior illustrated (lower picture) is from another Corbusier house, but one also planned with the principal

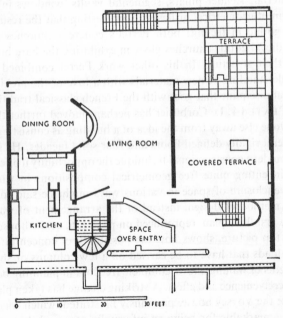

FIRST FLOOR PLAN OF A HOUSE AT GARCHES, NEAR PARIS, by Le Corbusier and Jeanneret. *See Plate 14 (top)*

rooms on the first floor, at which level this photograph is taken. It shows the staircase hall and part of the staircase itself, with a garden terrace, seen through the open door, connected with the garden by a ramp. It exemplifies again both the architect's fondness for airy, light, and spacious interiors and his reliance for architectural effect on the interplay of quite simple geometrical forms.

Houses by Le Corbusier belong to the category that take their effect from their contrast with nature. Instead of melting into their background like the natural materials of a stone-built farmhouse, the synthetic materials he uses – concrete, glass, and shining paint – are intended to detach themselves from their surroundings and make the most of their own brilliance. It is a sophisticated type of architecture that needs perfect finish to maintain its effect. It must always look elegantly new instead of mellowing with time.

PLATE 15. The Stockholm Exhibition of 1930 was an important landmark in the development of modern architecture. It was the first opportunity of seeing what a whole world of modern architecture might look like. The huge spaces enclosed only by glass set in a light frame, and the bold use of modern structural forms such as the cantilever, showed a large public for the first time the elegance of modern architecture as well as its efficiency. The exterior photograph illustrates the typical modern effect of walls and windows being a skin stretched on the light frame that supports them. The glass surface of the windows is flush with the walls instead of being more or less deeply recessed as in traditional masonry construction. This effect is enhanced by the thinness of window and door divisions, emphasizing their non-weight-bearing nature.

PLATE 16. The Paimio Tuberculosis Sanatorium is situated remotely in a pine forest in the interior of Finland. In this building reinforced concrete construction has produced not only the surface patterning of wall and window in the centre portion, but also the bold modelling of the end of the projecting wing, in which the actual bones of the framework of the lift shaft and the cantilevered balconies are exposed with dramatic effect. The ample ground available allowed the building to be informally planned, with the administrative portion as the core and wings radiating from it at whatever angle the direction of sun and view demanded.

PLATE 17. This famous school at Villejuif was built in 1932 by the only Communist municipality in Paris. The building is a careful piece of planning worked out from a detailed study of ideal school requirements. Reinforced concrete construction has been taken full advantage of, and the building is typical in its general lines of those that derive their appearance from this type of construction with its long spans and slender supports. Notice the way the main block of the building stands on legs, with the school playground running underneath, providing an outdoor playing space sheltered from the weather. Also the large windows giving ample light to the classrooms. They run continuously along the façades, being interrupted only by the thin cross-partition walls that also serve to brace the main structural framework. A corridor runs along the far side of the classrooms, separating them from the street. At right-angles to the main block is a one-storey nursery school, which is planned to protect the playground from the prevailing wind. Notice also the absence of pipes which, as in most modern buildings, are concealed within the structure.

PLATE 18. The Bergpolder flats at Rotterdam are a Dutch attempt to deal with a case where a large number of people have to be housed on a restricted site. By building a block nine storeys high as much of the ground area as possible is left free. The building occupies the centre of the area, leaving space all round so that plenty of light reaches even the lowest storeys. Very generous balconies running the full width of each flat allow the occupants to sit out in the open air. The horizontal lines of these balconies and the vertical screens separating each flat make an interesting pattern on the façade, aptly suggesting both the nature of the building (an assembly of identical units) and the cellular construction that allows continuous windows along the façade shown in the photograph. A large living-room and a bedroom alongside it occupy this side of each flat. Behind are another bedroom and a small kitchen and bathroom. At the near end of the building a tall glass-enclosed staircase and a lift give access to the balcony corridors which run along the far side of the building and off which the front doors open. Several small shops are grouped round the foot of the staircase.

The flats at Doldertal, Zurich (lower picture), are a more luxurious type and consist of three identical blocks each with one flat occupying a whole floor. As with several buildings already described, the living accommodation proper begins on the first floor, the ground floor being occupied by entrance hall, garages, and storage space. This is a sensible arrangement, particularly in a town or near the street, where ground-floor rooms are seldom very pleasant to inhabit, being more noisy and dusty than upper rooms and getting less light and view. The inclusion of the garage within the building has the added advantage that the car can be reached without going out of doors and is protected from frost by the warmth of the house. It is, however, not always practicable except with modern skeleton frame construction, which leaves the ground floor space sufficiently free from obstructions instead of being subdivided by solid walls supporting the walls of the rooms above. The structure in this case is a steel frame with light walls supported on the floors. This makes possible the generous balconies, reached from the living-room of each flat, uninterrupted by vertical supports.

PLATE 19. This gigantic government office building dominates a central quarter of Prague. Being of such a size it is content to get its effect by the rich surface pattern given by repetition of a standard office window and the sheen of the glazed tiles with which it is faced. The cruciform plan is a convenient one for an office building as each wing is equally accessible from the lift hall in the centre, and there are no gloomy courtyards, all offices looking outwards. The entrance is an appropriate use of cantilever construction.

PLATE 20. These two buildings were among the first skyscrapers to recapture the straightforward, expressive lines that tall office buildings had been given by Louis Sullivan and others in Chicago in the eighteen-eighties, but which had been lost when it became the fashion to dress them up with period-style decorations. Architects generally have now learnt the value of relying on the soaring lines of the structure and the rhythm of the hundreds of windows, adding to Sullivan's honesty of expression some of the sleekness of twentieth-century machine finishes – see also a later example, the Lever building, New York (Plate 40).

PLATE 21. This striking building, of reinforced concrete, raised on rows of pillars, was the first important work of modern architecture in Brazil, a country which has since revelled in architectural experiments. It is notable that it is a government office, as most governments are not willing to sponsor untried and unfamiliar styles of architecture. The façade shown is covered by a *brise-soleil* or louvred sunscreen, designed to interrupt the rays of the sun and prevent overheating and glare inside. This device, which works on the same principle as the Venetian blind, represents one of the few wholly new contributions that the modern style has made to the language of architecture. Le Corbusier, who was consulting architect for this building, was the first to design these louvred screens as an integral part, technically and aesthetically, of a building. The pattern of vertical and horizontal compartments, whose proportions are worked out to suit the direction and height of the sun, give depth and richness to the normally flat surface of the typical contemporary façade, and create a different set of rhythms from those produced by the alternation of wall and window which the *brise-soleil* conceals.

PLATE 22. This factory, designed by an engineer, was one of the first large-scale modern buildings in this country, but is still one of the best. It shows how ideally fitted 'mushroom' construction is for industrial buildings. This form of construction, as its name suggests, consists of reinforced concrete columns from which the concrete floor-slabs spring outwards in all directions. The floors are entirely supported by a row of these columns down each wing of the building, and the external walls, which carry no weight at all, are glass from floor to ceiling.

PLATE 23. Mention was made in Chapter VI of the high standard of design maintained by the London Passenger Transport Board, and of the good influence this work exercised on English architecture in the nineteen-twenties and nineteen-thirties. Arnos Grove is typical of the best of their suburban underground railway stations. It is dignified without being pompous, restrained without being too austere, and unmistakably English. It is a brick building with concrete roofs and a continuous concrete lintel to span the large windows of the circular booking hall. The photograph shows also the good design, simple but gracefully proportioned, of lamp standards and signs.

PLATE 24. Highpoint flats, on the highest point of Highgate Hill, have an interesting plan in the shape of a double cross with one flat occupying each arm of the cross on every floor and two occupying the middle, lifts and staircases being at the two intersections. This means that, with one exception, flats do not adjoin, so noise cannot be transmitted through partition walls. It also means that each flat can have cross ventilation.

Flats in this building are of two types (labelled A and B on the upper floor plan), both having a large living-room with a sliding window opening half the length of the room, but one type having two bedrooms and the other three bedrooms plus a separate dining-room. An interesting innovation is the provision of maids' bedrooms at ground floor level, which can be rented by tenants of the flats according to need and which give both maids and their employers that privacy in their leisure hours that the congested life of flats often denies them. Notice how the ground floor entrance hall is treated as a quite independent structure, the flats above being supported on columns within the hall. The building is of reinforced concrete panel construction; that is, walls and floors are continuous and homogeneous slabs of reinforced concrete. The walls are generally only four inches thick, but are insulated on the inside with slabs of cork.

PLATE 25. One of the joint architects of the Bexhill Pavilion, Erich Mendelsohn, was a leading architect in Germany until the Nazis came to power. This building was the result of a competition and an instance, rare at that time, of a municipal authority sponsoring modern architecture. It is a centre for all forms of seaside recreation and entertainment. The front of the building shown in the picture faces the sea and the tall windows of the lounge on the first floor and the restaurant below slide fully open in fine weather, when the terrace in front can be used as an open-air café. All parts of the building, which also contains a concert hall and a library, are connected by the glass-enclosed circular staircase from the terrace of which the photograph is taken.

The steel and concrete frame construction permits the very large window openings that the purpose of the building de-

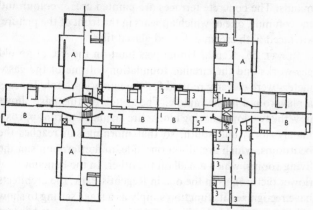

Upper Floor Plan

1. Living-room   3. Bedrooms   5. Kitchen   7. Entrance
2. Dining recess   4. Bathroom   6. W.C.   hall

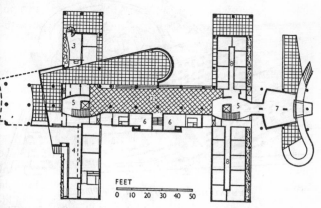

Ground Floor Plan

1. Hall and winter garden   5. Lifts and staircases
2. Hall   6. One-room flats
3. Porter's flat   7. Tea-room
4. Large flat   8. Maids' bedrooms

HIGHPOINT FLATS, LONDON, by Tecton. *See Plate 24*

mands. The concrete terraces are painted cream-colour and the columns, one of which appears in the front of the picture, are faced with cream-coloured glazed tiles.

PLATE 26. Kensal House was built on the site of an old gas-works and the circular foundations of one of the gasometers were cleverly re-used for the nursery school. There is a playground in the middle. The sketch on this page shows how the two long curving blocks are arranged to run approximately north and south, so that morning sun reaches the bedrooms, which are all on one side, and afternoon sun the living-rooms, which are all on the other. In the Penguin Pool (lower picture), as in the one in Regent's Park, the architects have recognized its function simply as a stage setting to show off the penguins' behaviour, and reinforced concrete has lent itself to the rather sculpturesque design demanded.

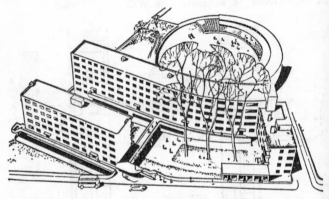

KENSAL HOUSE, LONDON. *See Plate 26.*

PLATE 27. A country house built entirely of timber. The garden front, shown in the photograph, is an open framework filled in with large windows, and the other sides are faced with cedar boarding. As the plans show, all the principal rooms are ranged along the garden side, the bedrooms on the upper floor being set back to provide a continuous balcony. The garden terrace running at right angles to the house, sheltered from the wind and from being overlooked from the drive by a brick wall, terminates in a trellis-work screen that echoes the design of the garden façade. The lower panels of the screen are filled with plate-glass, also to break the wind. The interior view shows the effect of sliding the glass windows of the living-room aside to throw it open to the terrace. See plans on pages 146 and 147.

PLATE 28. Steel and glass used with dramatic effect for purposes of display. A spiral staircase of steel is enclosed in a glass drum with a showcase half-way up, the goods in which can be seen from both inside and out. This photograph is taken by night, and also shows an effective use of neon lighting, which nowadays often plays an important part in exterior design.

PLATE 29. The modern department store needs more than anything else the maximum possible uninterrupted floor-space for displaying and selling merchandise. And steel-

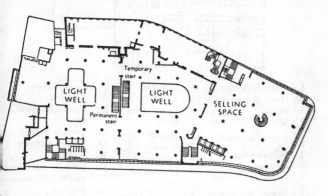

TYPICAL FLOOR PLAN, PETER JONES STORE, SLOANE SQUARE, by William Crabtree (with Slater and Moberley and C. H. Reilly). *See Plate 29.*

frame construction, as the typical floor-plan of this building shows, is capable of reducing the amount of space taken up by the structure to a few remarkably small points. The external walls are screen walls only, as the weight-bearing stanchions are set inside the face of the wall. This gives uninterrupted window-space. The wall-space is divided into equal units by vertical ribs. The space between the rows of windows is faced with glass which is hinged like the windows

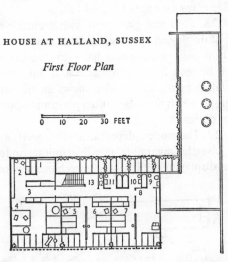

HOUSE AT HALLAND, SUSSEX

First Floor Plan

0   10   20   30 FEET

1. Owner's bathroom	13. Stair hall	25. Garden store
2.⎫ Owner's dressing-	14. Vestibule	26. Laundry
3.⎭ room	15. Cloak-room	27. Garage for three
4. Owner's bedroom	16. W.C.	cars
5.⎫ Guests' rooms	17. Shower	28. Terrace store
6.⎭	18. Study	29. Service entrance
7. Night nursery	19. Living-room	30. Larder
8. Day nursery	20. Dining-room	31. Servants' bathroom
9. Nursery bathroom	21. Pool	and W.C.
10.⎫ Guests' bathrooms	22.⎫ Servants' rooms	32. Kitchen
11.⎭	23.⎭	33. Servants' sitting
12. W.C.	24. Water purifica-	space
	tion plant	34. Hall

so that its coloured backing can be changed at will. The whole building thus has an easily-cleaned surface.

PLATE 30. A new type of municipal building in which all the health services of the Borough of Finsbury are centralized. The diagrams on page 149 show how the different functions of the building are planned so as not to interfere with one

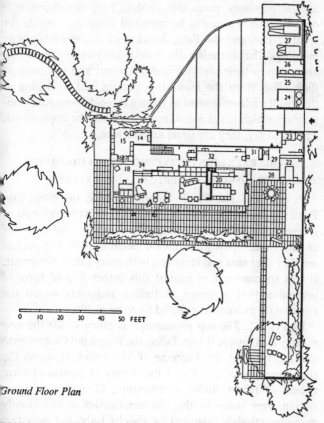

0 10 20 30 40 50 FEET

Ground Floor Plan

HOUSE AT HALLAND, SUSSEX, by Serge Chermayeff. *See Plate 27.*

another. The photograph shows one wing of the symmetrical plan. The concrete frame, consisting of roof-slabs and a solid end wall to take all the horizontal stresses, is faced with glazed tiles. The intermediate floor is supported on box-shaped beams running the length of the building. The space inside them, below the upper row of windows, and the equivalent space below the lower windows, is used to take all the necessary pipes and cables. They are faced with opaque glass which can be removed from the outside for repairs. This and the Peter Jones store are essentially city buildings. They are finished in smooth easily washed materials, are urban in their sophisticated character, and get much of their effect from the interesting pattern and modelling of their wall surfaces instead of from a three-dimensional composition which needs a distant viewpoint to be appreciated. That is to say, they are street architecture.

SOME REPRESENTATIVE MODERN BUILDINGS
IN EUROPE, AMERICA, AND BRITAIN

PLATE 31. The Pirelli building, Milan (architect Gio Ponti; engineer, Pier Luigi Nervi) is the most remarkable of several beautifully finished office buildings in that centre of architectural sophistication. Completed in 1960, it is the last word in sleekness and elegance, with every detail consistent. It was to some extent against this rather limited form of perfection that a group of Italian architects staged the reactionary movement referred to on page 106.

PLATE 32. The top photograph is taken inside the new railway terminus at Rome, facing the Piazza dei Cinquecento and the ruins of the Thermae of Diocletian. It shows the slick precision of finish and the clarity of structural form typical of recent Italian architecture. Designs for a new station were made in the nineteen-thirties in the heavily monumental style favoured by Fascist Italy, but only two

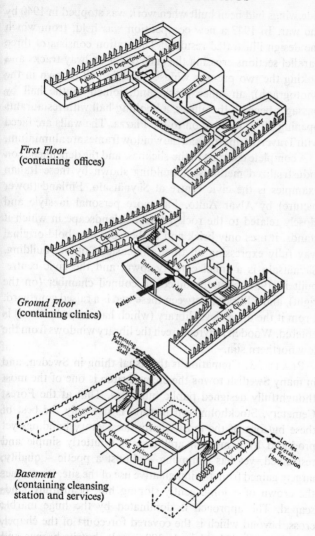

First Floor
(containing offices)

Public Health Department

Lecture Hall

Terrace

Reception House

Caretaker

Ground Floor
(containing clinics)

Foot

Dental

Women's

Lav

El Treatment

Entrance

Hall

Lav

Patients

Tuberculosis Clinic

Basement
(containing cleansing station and services)

Cleansing Patients Staff

Archives

Disinfection

Cleansing Station

Mortuary

Lorries Caretaker & Reception House

FINSBURY HEALTH CENTRE, by Tecton. *See Plate 30.*

side wings had been built when work was stopped in 1940 by the war. In 1947 a new competition was held, from which the design illustrated resulted. The station consists of three parallel sections crossing the ends of the railway tracks and linking the two pre-war wings: a public hall (shown in the photograph), an office block, and, joined to the hall by passages beneath the offices, a booking-hall with restaurants opening off it, looking on to the Piazza. The walls are faced with Travertine marble and the window frames are aluminium.

A complete contrast to the slickness and the dependence on industrialized methods of building shown by these Italian examples is the civic centre at Säynätsalo, Finland (lower picture) by Alvar Aalto. Far more personal in style and closely related to the rocky, forested landscape in which it stands, it uses only brick and timber, but in a bold original way fully expressing all three dimensions of the building. Säynätsalo is a small country town, and the civic centre, built in 1951, contains offices, a council chamber (on the right), and a library. Between these two is a raised courtyard. From it the upper-level library (which has shops below it) is entered. Wooden louvres screen the library windows from the low northern sun.

PLATE 33. Cremation is the usual thing in Sweden, and in many Swedish towns the crematorium is one of the most thoughtfully designed public buildings. That at the Forest Cemetery, Stockholm, top picture, is not only the best of these but one of the most wholly satisfactory buildings yet produced by a modern architect. It is utterly simple and restrained, yet has a moving – almost a poetic – quality, largely gained from the imaginative use of the site. It occupies the crown of a long, gently sloping hill, beautifully landscaped. The approach is dominated by the huge marble cross, beyond which is the covered forecourt of the chapel. The chapel itself holds only 300 people, but its bronze and glass doors can be lowered into the ground, allowing a far greater number, standing in the columned forecourt seen in

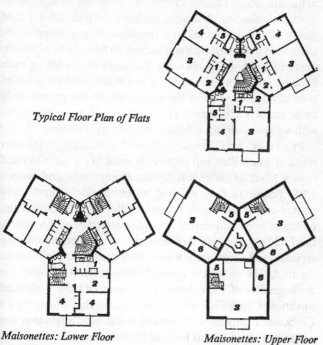

Typical Floor Plan of Flats

Maisonettes: Lower Floor

Maisonettes: Upper Floor

1. Kitchen
2. Dining-room
3. Living-room
4. Bedroom
5. Clothes cupboard
6. Store

FLATS AT GRONDAL, STOCKHOLM, by Backström and Reinius, *See Plate 33.*

the picture, to take part in the services. This is the most notable work of Sweden's greatest architect, who died, aged only fifty-five, soon after it was finished.

The flats shown in the lower picture have the qualities found in all the better Swedish housing schemes: a straightforward yet homely architectural character, an unselfconscious use of traditional as well as modern, industrially produced, materials, and a carefully worked out relationship to the site, which ensures variety and humanity. A number of blocks of identical Y-shape, designed to give all the flats plenty of sun and to avoid a troublesome prevailing wind, are spaced well apart on a site sloping up from Lake Mälaren, west of Stockholm. Each wing contains a single flat on each floor or maisonettes occupying two floors, and on a lower ground floor of some of the blocks, where the ground falls away steeply, are shops. The walls are of concrete blocks with a plaster surface colour-washed in light shades.

PLATE 34. Le Corbusier's *Unité d'Habitation* on the outskirts of Marseilles, top picture, is more like a town in itself than a block of flats. It is sixteen storeys high and houses 1,600 people in flats planned on either side of artificially lighted corridors, which on certain floors, half-way up the building, become internal shopping streets. Besides shops, the building contains day nurseries and other community services, and a gymnasium and other recreation facilities on the roof. The flats have aroused much interest not only for the ingenuity of their detailed planning and the sculptural qualities of the building itself, but because they exemplify Le Corbusier's principles of vertical living, which however are not to be judged by this isolated building because it was conceived as one of a group of similar tall blocks, spaced wide apart in open parkland and linked by community buildings, plantations, and roadways.

The pilgrimage chapel of Notre-Dame-du-Haut at Ronchamp, perched on a spur of the Vosges – a replacement of a war-damaged chapel – represents one of the many occasions when the great French architect Le Corbusier has astonished the world of architecture (as Picasso has repeatedly astonished the world of painting) by producing something apparently quite unrelated to his previous line of development

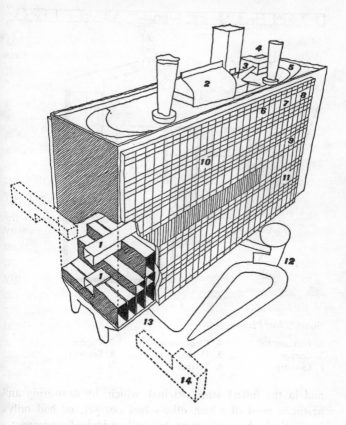

1. Internal thoroughfare
2. Gymnasium
3. Café and sun terrace
4. Cafeteria
5. Children's playground
6. Health centre
7. Crèche
8. Nursery
9. Club
10. Youth clubs and workshops
11. Communal laundry and drying rooms
12. Entrance and porter's lodge
13. Garages
14. Standard two-floor flat

FLATS AT MARSEILLES, by Le Corbusier. *See Plate 33.*

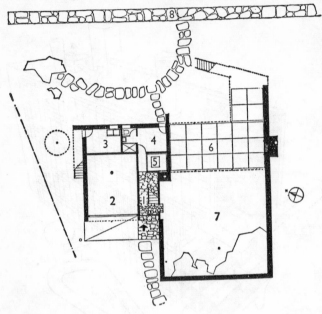

Ground Floor Plan

1. Entrance hall
2. Garage
3. Laundry
4. Cloak-room
5. Heating
6. Terrace
7. Garden
8. Sea wall

and in the fullest sense original, which, by answering an aesthetic need of which others had not yet, or had only instinctively, become aware, has had an immediate impact. The chapel, completed in 1955, has as much the character of sculpture as of architecture and is an exceedingly personal building, full of subtle experiments in the use of light and form and colour.

PLATE 35. This is part of a business training college at Heidelberg, Germany (architect, F. W. Kraemer) built in 1957. It is the kind of simple, unpretentious architecture that

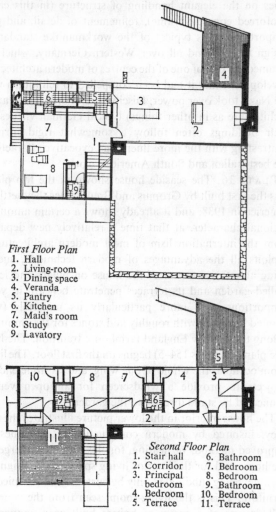

First Floor Plan
1. Hall
2. Living-room
3. Dining space
4. Veranda
5. Pantry
6. Kitchen
7. Maid's room
8. Study
9. Lavatory

Second Floor Plan
1. Stair hall
2. Corridor
3. Principal bedroom
4. Bedroom
5. Terrace
6. Bathroom
7. Bedroom
8. Bedroom
9. Bathroom
10. Bedroom
11. Terrace

HOUSE AT COHASSET, MASS. by Walter Gropius and Marcel Breuer. *See Plate 36.*

relies on the elegant handling of structure (in this case a reinforced concrete frame), refinement of detail, and good proportions. It is typical of the workmanlike standard of design to be found all over Western Germany, which has resumed the role of one of the centres of modern architectural development that it had been compelled to relinquish when the Nazis took over power. Discipline and orderliness are (in architecture as in other things) typical German virtues, but their buildings often follow a somewhat rigid formula, contrasting with the more fluent and evocative character of the best Italian and South American work.

PLATE 36. The seaside house shown in the top picture was the first built by Gropius and Breuer after they settled in America in 1938, and it already shows a certain amount of regional character, at that time a relatively new departure from the internationalism of most modern architecture. It exploits all the advantages of modern technique, such as being able to raise part of the house on pillars and let the walled garden and its terraces penetrate beneath it, yet its proportions, and more particularly its materials (white painted boarding with roughly laid stones for the chimneys), belong to the New England farmhouse tradition. The house (see plans on pages 154–5) begins on the first floor. The living-room occupies the whole of one wing, and its stone end wall projects to provide a windscreen for an open veranda connected by stairs directly to the garden.

The house interior in the lower picture illustrates the tendency, inspired by modern constructional techniques and improved methods of heating, for the garden to merge into the house and for the interior living space to be designed as a whole, being subdivided only by curtains and low pieces of furniture. This is the living-room, seen from the staircase-hall, in one of a group of houses built as a cooperative enterprise by this young architectural partnership, for their own occupation or that of other young couples, mostly staff from the neighbouring Harvard University.

PLATE 37. Typical of the style of house evolved by

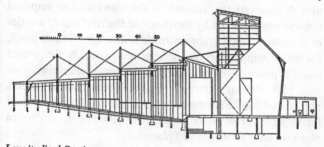

Longitudinal Section
OPERA HOUSE AT STOCKBRIDGE, MASS, by Saarinen, Swanson, and Saarinen. *See Plate 39.*

modern architects on the Pacific side of the United States, where the sub-tropical climate allows a partly outdoor life and much is made of garden terraces as extensions of the living-room, shaded by overhanging roofs. Neutra is especially skilful in blending the local landscape and vegetation with its freely planned houses, terraces, and gardens. Screen walls shelter the terraces from the prevailing winds.

PLATE 38. Taliesin West was the winter home (as Taliesin, Wisconsin, was the summer home) of Frank Lloyd Wright and his disciple-apprentices. It was largely built by his apprentices themselves, in between studying with the Master and working on his buildings and projects. A romantic conception, occupying a rocky site in the open desert, it is constructed of rough concrete, with coloured local boulders embedded in it, of baulks of timber and canvas for the roofs: another instance of climate and a way of living inspiring an architect to whom every problem was a challenge to produce a work of real originality and power.

PLATE 39. The top building, an opera shed for the productions of a local music centre, has a rural setting and holds an audience of 1,200. It is all of timber, unpainted. The shape of the auditorium is based on acoustical needs, which also determined the volume of the interior. The required volume was achieved by constructing the roof out of a series of laminated wood arches with tie beams across their bases, the latter supporting the ceiling, above which the arches stand exposed. The ceiling is stepped down (see drawing on page 157), also for acoustical reasons. The proscenium arch is hinged and can be swung back when the building is required for concerts. The whole stage then becomes an orchestra platform with room for 110 players.

The lower picture shows one of the many buildings designed during the last fifteen years or so by Mies van der Rohe for the Illinois Institute of Technology in Chicago. They, together with the Lake Shore Drive apartments in Chicago, the Seagram building in New York (designed with Philip Johnson), and a few private houses, constitute the bulk of the work he has carried out since he left Germany for the United States just before the war; but though relatively small in quantity it has been very influential – see pages 110–11. This example illustrates many of the qualities associated with his work, especially his utter reliance on proportion and finish. The role of each constituent – the steel frame, the brick panels, the wall-glazing – can be separately apprehended, and each is finished with the precision that belongs to machine engineering, evoking the same sort of aesthetic satisfaction as a neatly balanced mathematical equation.

PLATE 40. Sheathed in stainless steel and blue-green heat-resisting glass, this building is one of America's key contributions to the process by which the architecture of tall city buildings has come increasingly to consist of beautiful finishes applied to sleek unadorned geometry. Apart from its dramatic visual qualities, the special interest of this building lies in the use it makes of a closely built-up city site. The ground area, partly planted as a garden, is open to the public. Except for an open courtyard in the centre it is roofed by a single floor of offices from one side of which rises the main building of twenty-four storeys, occupying considerably less of its site than by-laws permit and therefore admitting an unusual amount of air and light to the surrounding streets – the only way of planning really high buildings if a gloomy effect of deep canyon-streets is to be avoided and good working conditions provided even in the lower office floors.

PLATE 41. The brilliant achievements of the modern architects of Brazil (see page 107) have largely been individual ones, in which social planning has played but little part; but an exception is this new residential neighbourhood on the outskirts of Rio, designed for the lower-paid municipal workers. On a 12-acre site, about 2,400 people are housed in four blocks of flats and provided with a community centre, a health centre, shops and a market, a primary school, and various sports buildings.

The upper picture shows the end wall of the gymnasium attached to the primary school in the same neighbourhood. Its concrete roof displays the vigorous curves beloved by several of the leading Brazilian architects, and it is faced with *azuleijos*, or coloured tiles, painted or arranged in patterns, a favourite form of decoration inherited by the Brazilians from their Portuguese forebears. The President's palace in the new capital city of Brasilia (lower picture) shows Brazil's most famous architect, Oscar Niemeyer, handling his favourite curving forms with a new maturity and control. This view is taken looking along the veranda which fronts the palace, towards the snail-shaped reinforced concrete private chapel that stands on a platform near the end of the building. The outer face of the veranda has a screen consisting

159

of inverted arches of white marble, with their surfaces subtly faceted and their edges subtly moulded, which partially supports the roof and casts welcome patches of shade on the veranda floor. The palace was completed in 1958, the first major building at Brasilia, which became the official capital of the country in 1960. It stands on the edge of an artificial lake formed by damming a couple of streams. The lake provides a head of water for hydro-electric power.

PLATE 42. Nearly fifty schools were completed by Hertfordshire County Council between 1946 and 1952, an achievement made possible by planning each school in multiples or subdivisions of one standard dimension and mass-producing structural components and wall-units to fit it. The units are small enough to allow each school to adapt itself to different requirements and site conditions, yet large enough to allow rapid assembly on the site, to which the appropriate numbers of the various standard types of unit are delivered from a central depot, itself kept supplied from the factories. The structural unit is a light steel frame with lattice beams, and the walling unit a pre-cast concrete slab. In certain places panels of mild steel, painted, are used instead. In Hertfordshire these materials have been used in a sufficiently imaginative way to produce a style of architecture of unusual lightness and grace, with airy interiors largely formed of transparent partitions varied by solid panels finished in bright colours. The informal planning of the post-war English school aptly reflects the needs of the English public education system in its transitional state, following recent legislation. The architects clearly found it stimulating to work in cooperation with educationists who were as much in an experimental mood as they were. The standard plan-dimension of these schools was at first 8 ft 3 in. (which, divided by three, gave the standard-size window or door, as the upper photograph clearly shows), but later a smaller unit of only 3 ft 4 in. was tried, and found preferable as giving more freedom to the designer.

PLATE 43. The picture shows one of the first blocks to be completed in a large housing scheme, comprising flats and maisonettes with a number of shops and small community buildings, begun after the war by the Westminster City Council. It was the subject of a competition. The thirty-acre site was an area of obsolete terrace housing, much damaged by bombing, on the north bank of the Thames. Across the river lies Battersea power station, and surplus heat from this, in the form of hot water which would otherwise be discharged into the river and wasted, is pumped through a tunnel beneath the river and used to heat the whole housing scheme. It is stored in the glass-enclosed tower seen at the far end of the flats, from which it is distributed to the various blocks. The nine-storey block illustrated contains 104 flats reached by glass-walled staircases projecting from the other side, and by lifts. They are concrete-frame structures, with external walls of yellow brick enlivened by brightly coloured paint inside the recessed balconies.

PLATE 44. The South Bank Exhibition of 1951 gave the younger British architects, normally restricted at that time to utilitarian activities, the chance to show what liveliness and gaiety modern architecture is capable of, given the opportunity. It was also invaluable as a full-scale exercise in urban planning, and its planning is more likely to have a lasting influence on architecture in Britain than the design of its buildings. Previous exhibitions, even the most epoch-making, had remained formal and conventional in layout. At the South Bank Exhibition, by contrast, the buildings were grouped in irregular fashion round a series of court-yards, permitting a great variety of scale and character. Changes of level and floor-surface, informal planting, the elements of concealment and surprise – in fact all the tradi-

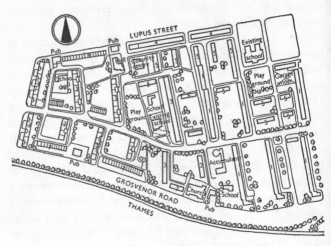

Site Plan

1. 9-storey flats
2. 11-storey flats
3. 10-storey flats

4. 7-storey flats
5. 4-storey flats

6. 4-storey flats
7. 3-storey houses

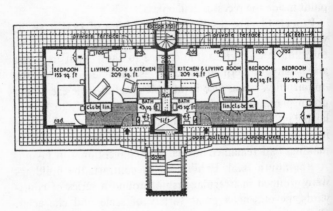

Plan of Typical Flats (Scale $\frac{1}{16}$ in. = 1 ft 0 in.)
HOUSING IN WESTMINSTER, by Powell and Moya. *See Plate 43.*

162

tional devices employed by the Picturesque landscape planners of the eighteenth century – were consciously used here for the first time in an urban setting. The London skyline across the river and the views of the towers of Westminster obtainable from the site were skilfully incorporated into the

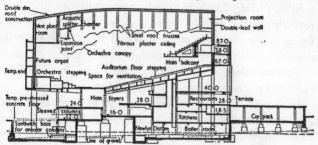

Longitudinal Section (Scale 1 in.=80 ft 0 in.)

ROYAL FESTIVAL HALL, LONDON, by Robert Matthew, architect to the London County Council, J. L. Martin, deputy architect, Edwin Williams, and Peter Moro. *See Plate 45.*

exhibition's scenic effects, showing how newly designed areas can be woven, as it were, into the fabric of existing cities. The South Bank was due to be laid out permanently during the subsequent years, and the principles of town design tried out in the exhibition suggested the form this layout might take. Unfortunately these hopes have not been fulfilled. Another important feature of the exhibition was the care given to the minor details of outdoor design – lamp-posts, railings, seats, steps, signs, planting, and the like – which form an important part of any architectural effect but often lie outside the architect's control.

PLATE 45. The Royal Festival Hall occupies a particularly difficult site from the point of view of noise, being alongside Hungerford railway bridge, but the architects and engineers have successfully excluded all external sounds from the main auditorium by giving it double walls and a double roof of reinforced concrete, and surrounding it with foyers and staircases and, overlooking the River Thames, with restaurants, which provide an additional sound barrier. Immense pains were taken with the internal acoustics to give the maximum definition and brilliance of tone. The auditorium, seating 3,000, is raised on columns with the main foyer beneath it, which allows crowds to be quickly distributed to the entrances at the different levels. The aesthetic possibilities of this type of planning, which modern methods of construction specially encourage, are imaginatively exploited to create impressive effects of space internally.

PLATE 46. This rubber factory is part of a new industrial area planned after the war in a remote Welsh valley, and has its own housing nearby. It is a notable example of the way the modern architect can become an ally of the enterprising manufacturer by designing a building based on close analysis of the sequence of operations that has to take place in it, with resulting efficiency and economy; also of the bold use of reinforced concrete construction, including a then fairly new technique called shell-concrete. This enables large spaces (in this factory the main production area) to be covered by shallow domes – incidentally reintroducing curving lines into modern architecture, which had hitherto been specially identified with straight lines.

PLATE 47. A school and an office-building, both frame structures with the main accommodation on the upper floor and deriving their architectural character from the boldness with which this form of construction is expressed and from the rhythmical subdivision of the large windows that improved methods of heating make possible nowadays. In the school the classrooms are planned in a square surrounding a high-roofed central assembly-hall. The offices (which are for an engineering company and adjoin the company's factory) are also planned round a square, in this case with an open

courtyard in the centre. On the ground floor are administrative offices and on the first floor, lit by continuous aluminium windows, the main designing and drawing offices. The
walling below the upper range of windows is of coloured
glass panels, and in the centre, in an aluminium frame, is a
decorative panel made from local pebbles and fossils. It is
only recently that industrial buildings have been considered
suitable for embellishment of this kind; previously grime and
squalor were considered inseparable from industry.

PLATE 48. An important British post-war contribution to
housing is the kind of mixed development planned by the
London County Council architects in their Roehampton
estates on the south-west fringe of London, alongside
Richmond Park. They are built on the large gardens of
obsolete Victorian mansions, so there are plenty of well-
grown trees. Among these (left picture) stand tall blocks of
flats and maisonettes, between which are lower blocks and
rows of small houses, the whole catering for many sizes and
types of family with varying needs, and creating at the same
time an informal pattern of buildings woven into the landscape.

The passenger building at Britain's newest major airport,
at Gatwick, Sussex (right picture), makes bold and expressive
use of typical modern structural materials: a reinforced
concrete frame for the lower part, backed by a brick screen
wall, and steel and glass curtain-walling above. The latter
encloses the main concourse, which is at an upper level,
spanning the London–Brighton road (foreground of picture)
and reached by car by means of spiral concrete ramps on
the far side of the building. On the left is the 900 ft long
'finger' – a covered passage along which passengers walk to
the waiting aircraft. It passes over various administrative
and service buildings. Architects, Yorke, Rosenberg, and
Mardall.

BIBLIOGRAPHY

BIBLIOGRAPHY

THE following list of works in which the subject of this book can be studied in greater detail is divided into four sections: first, books dealing with the history and social background of modern architecture; secondly, books dealing with modern buildings themselves; thirdly, books dealing with town-planning (whose close relationship with modern architecture makes the understanding of one essential to the other); and, fourthly, periodicals. The list, which is arranged in alphabetical order according to the names of the authors, is generally confined to English books, though a few others are included where no equivalent is available in English. The date given is that of first publication. The list does not pretend to be inclusive, but only to select the most useful books on each subject. Purely technical textbooks are omitted. A number of the books listed are now out of print, but they can be found at public libraries.

1. HISTORY AND BACKGROUND

Badmin, S. R. *Village and Town*. Penguin Books, 1942.

A children's picture-book, but one that gives a clear summary of the regional, technical, and social origins of different styles of architecture.

Banham, Reyner. *Theory and Design in the First Machine Age*. London: The Architectural Press, 1960.

A scholarly and stimulating study of the emergence of modern architecture and of the revolutionary art movements to which it is related.

Betjeman, John. *Ghastly Good Taste*. London: Chapman and Hall, 1933.

An entertaining and sometimes savage analysis of the taste prevailing at the time, stressing its social background.

Blomfield, Sir Reginald. *Richard Norman Shaw*. London: B. T. Batsford, 1941.

Gives useful information about an architect whose influence was – and still is – immense, but has the defect of being written from a very prejudiced point of view. The author largely misinterprets the importance of Shaw's work.

BIBLIOGRAPHY

Boumphrey, Geoffrey. *Your House and Mine*. London: Allen and Unwin, 1938.

An interesting historical survey of house-building and the styles of living that different types of house represent. Starting with primitive times, it leads up to discussion of modern needs and means.

Gibberd, Frederick. *The Architecture of England*. London: The Architectural Press, 1938 (since revised).

A very condensed but well-illustrated history of English architecture, which takes proper note of causes as well as effects. It takes the story right up to the present day, which is a thing most conventional histories avoid doing. They usually stop at the beginning of last century just when developments were becoming interesting in relation to our own day.

Giedion, Sigfried. *Space, Time and Architecture*. Harvard University Press; Oxford University Press, 1941.

A most important, if rather difficult, book on the evolution of modern architecture and town-planning, from a philosophical standpoint.

Hatje, Gerd (edited by). *Encyclopaedia of Modern Architecture*. London: Thames and Hudson, 1963.

A useful dictionary of people and events.

Hitchcock, Henry-Russell. *Architecture: Nineteenth and Twentieth Centuries*. Penguin Books, 1958.

The most comprehensive analysis of the successive stylistic changes, and the influence of successive personalities, that have determined the outward form of buildings since the Georgian rule was relaxed.

Howarth, Thomas. *Mackintosh and the Modern Movement*. London: Routledge and Kegan Paul, 1952.

An exhaustive study of the great Scottish architect who was one of the pioneers of modern architecture at the end of the nineteenth century, and whose work had a great influence throughout Europe.

Joedicke, Jurgen. *A History of Modern Architecture*. London: The Architectural Press, 1958.

Translated from the German. Thorough and objective.

Klingender, F. D. *Art and the Industrial Revolution*. London: Noel Carrington, 1947.

A beautifully illustrated book giving the social and technical background out of which the necessity for a new architecture emerged.

BIBLIOGRAPHY

Lancaster, Osbert. *Pillar to Post*. London: John Murray, 1938.

Lancaster, Osbert. *Homes Sweet Homes*. London: John Murray, 1939.

Two satirical books, brilliantly illustrated, on the variegated styles of architecture of yesterday and today. The first deals with exteriors; the second with interiors.

Lethaby, W. R. *Form in Civilization*. Oxford University Press, 1922.

A collection of essays and lectures by the wisest of all English architectural writers. Though his name is seldom heard now, Lethaby was one of the few writers of good sense about architecture during the first quarter of this century, and we owe a great deal today to his teaching.

Lethaby, W. R. *Philip Webb and His Work*. Oxford University Press, 1935.

Mackail, J. W. *The Life of William Morris*. London: Longmans, Green and Co., 1922.

Mumford, Lewis (edited by). *Roots of Contemporary American Architecture*. New York: Reinhold, 1952.

A most revealing anthology of American writings about architecture from the mid nineteenth century onwards, with an introduction by the editor, tracing the evolution of modern architectural ideas in the U.S.A.

Mumford, Lewis. *Technics and Civilization*. London: George Routledge and Son, 1934.

A very important book by America's leading architectural critic and historian. It is a comprehensive history of machines and machinery as an increasingly significant element in human life, and shows how the quality of our present-day civilization depends on our learning to make proper use of machines. It contains an exhaustive bibliography filling twenty-seven pages.

Pevsner, Nikolaus. *An Outline of European Architecture*. Penguin Books, 1942 (since revised. Enlarged edition: John Murray. De Luxe edition: Penguin Books, 1960.)

An excellent history, which gives a great deal of information in a small space without becoming a mere catalogue.

Pevsner, Nikolaus. *Pioneers of Modern Design*. Penguin Books, 1960. (A revised and largely rewritten edition of *Pioneers of the Modern Movement*, Faber and Faber, 1936, reprinted by the Museum of

Modern Art, New York, in 1950, under the title *Pioneers of Modern Design*.)

A historical study of modern architecture in a largely biographical form. It deals comprehensively with the period from William Morris to Walter Gropius, but goes back earlier than Morris to describe the influence of early nineteenth-century engineering.

Quennell, Marjorie and C. H. B. *A History of Everyday Things in England*. London: B. T. Batsford, 1930–4. Four volumes.

A popular book (written specially for children, but of general interest) whose title explains itself.

Rasmussen, Steen Eiler. *Towns and Buildings*. Liverpool University Press, 1951.

A series of essays by Denmark's leading architectural critic, charmingly illustrated by the author, analysing the character of various cities past and present in relation to the way of life they represent.

Richards, J. M. *The Castles on the Ground*. London: The Architectural Press, 1946.

A study of the ordinary man's architectural environment which attempts to discover what he requires that contemporary architecture should offer him.

Richards, J. M. *The Functional Tradition in Early Industrial Buildings*. London: The Architectural Press, 1958.

A study, mostly in pictures (taken by Eric de Maré), of the largely anonymous functional buildings of the late eighteenth and nineteenth centuries – warehouses, docks, textile mills, breweries, and the like – with special reference to their affinities with modern architecture.

Richards, J. M. *A Miniature History of the English House*. London: The Architectural Press, 1938.

What its name suggests. Very brief and chiefly pictorial.

Schmutzler, Robert. *Art Nouveau*. London: Thames and Hudson, 1964.

An expensive but beautifully presented history of this short-lived but highly significant episode.

Sharp, T. *English Panorama*. London: The Architectural Press, 1950.

Revised version of a book published in 1936, which analyses the development of the English urban and rural scene through the centuries, and ends with a penetrating study of contemporary town-planning problems.

Steegman, John. *The Rule of Taste*. London: Macmillan, 1936.

A charmingly written account of aristocratic culture and taste from the period of George I to that of George IV. It explains particularly well the circumstances in which the fashion for antique styles arose at the end of the eighteenth century, and brings the story up to the Reform Bill of 1832.

Sullivan, Louis. *Kindergarten Chats*. Chicago: Scarab Press, 1934.

A mixture of autobiography and architectural philosophy from this great American pioneer of the eighteen-eighties.

Trappes-Lomax, M. *Pugin*. London: Sheed and Ward, 1932.

World Architecture: an illustrated history. London: Paul Hamlyn, 1963.

A lavish and beautifully illustrated volume by various authors. The modern section is by John Jacobus.

Wright, Frank Lloyd. *A Testament*. London: The Architectural Press, 1959.

The great American master's own picture of his work and ideas. Fully and excellently illustrated.

2. MODERN BUILDINGS: THEORY AND PRACTICE

Alvar Aalto. Zurich: Girsberger, 1963.

A full account, supervised by Aalto himself, of the work of this unique Finnish master.

Banham, Reyner. *Guide to Modern Architecture*. London: Architectural Press, 1962.

Blake, Peter. *The Master Builders*. London: Victor Gollancz, 1960.

A triple biography: of Le Corbusier, Mies van der Rohe, and Frank Lloyd Wright. A lively and readable account of their careers, achievements, and influence on each other.

Dannatt, Trevor (edited by). *Modern Architecture in Britain*. London: B. T. Batsford, 1959.

A photographic anthology of the best examples up to 1956, based on the exhibition of the same title held by the Arts Council in that year. It has an unusually lucid, analytical introduction by Sir John Summerson.

BIBLIOGRAPHY

Donat, John. *World Architecture: one*. London: Studio Books, 1964.

Illustrations and discussions of the newest modern buildings.

Giedion, S. (edited by). *C.I.A.M.; A Decade of New Architecture*. Zurich: Girsberger, 1951.

Illustrations of the best work of the members of the Congrès Internationaux d'Architecture Moderne for the first ten years after its foundation in 1928. Text in English, French, and German.

Giedion, S. *Walter Gropius*. London: The Architectural Press, 1954.

A well illustrated account of his life and work.

Gropius, Walter (trans. by P. Morton Shand). *The New Architecture and the Bauhaus*. London: Faber and Faber, 1935.

Gropius's own account of his ideas on architecture and architectural training and of the famous *Bauhaus* School at Dessau where he put his ideas into practice.

Hitchcock, Henry-Russell. *In the Nature of Materials*. New York: Duell, Sloan and Pearce, 1942. (English edition, Paul Elek, 1949.)

By far the best and completest account of the work of America's greatest architect, Frank Lloyd Wright.

Johnson, Philip. *Mies van der Rohe*. New York: Museum of Modern Art, 1947.

Lambert, Sam. *New Architecture of London*. British Travel and Holidays Association, 1963.

A useful inexpensive handbook listing worthwhile buildings put up since 1930.

Le Corbusier (trans. by Frederick Etchells). *Towards a New Architecture*. London: John Rodker, 1927, re-issued by the Architectural Press, 1947.

The great master's dramatically presented ideas about an ideal modern architecture and its relation to modern life. This book was for many people the first and exciting statement of the idea of a machine-age architecture.

Masters of World Architecture series. London: Mayflower, 1960.

Compact books, very well illustrated, on the work of major modern architects, each with a knowledgeable introduction. The first six volumes published are: *Le Corbusier*, by Françoise Choay; *Frank Lloyd*

Wright, by Vincent Scully (a particularly perceptive introduction); *Pier Luigi Nervi*, by Ada Louise Huxtable; *Antonio Gaudì*, by George R. Collins; *Ludwig Mies van der Rohe*, by Arthur Drexler; *Alvar Aalto*, by Frederick Gutheim.

Masters of Contemporary Architecture series. London: Prentice Hall International, 1962.

Similar to the above. The five volumes are on *R. Buckminster Fuller*, by John McHale; *Philip Johnson*, by John Jacobus; *Louis Kahn*, by Vincent Scully; *Kenzo Tange*, by Robin Boyd; and *Eero Saarinen*, by Allan Temko.

McCallum, Ian. *Architecture U.S.A.* London: The Architectural Press, 1958.

A well-chosen and well-illustrated anthology of the best recent American buildings, with brief biographies of their architects.

Mindlin, Henrique. *Modern Architecture in Brazil*. London: The Architectural Press, 1956.

A fully illustrated record of Brazil's very important contribution to modern architecture, up to the date of publication.

New German Architecture. London: The Architectural Press, 1956.

Illustrations of the best post-war work, selected and annotated by various hands.

Papadaki, Stamo (edited by). *Le Corbusier: architect, painter, writer.* New York: Macmillan, 1948.

Chronological account of the French master's works; mostly pictorial but with brief biographical and descriptive texts.

Papadaki, Stamo (edited by). *The Work of Oscar Niemeyer.* New York: Reinhold, 1950.

Richards, J. M. *An Architectural Journey in Japan.* London: The Architectural Press, 1963.

An account of the new architecture emerging from this rapidly developing country.

Richards, J. M. *Modern Architecture in Finland.* London: Finnish Travel Information Centre, 1964.

A booklet listing the most worthwhile buildings.

Smith, G. E. Kidder. *Sweden Builds*. London: The Architectural Press, 1950.

A comprehensive picture of Sweden's contribution to modern architecture, with the author's magnificent photographs, A very intelligent introductory section summarizes the historical, social, and topographical background.

Smith, G. E. Kidder. *Switzerland Builds*. London: The Architectural Press, 1950.

Similar to *Sweden Builds*.

Smith, G. E. Kidder. *Italy Builds*. London: The Architectural Press, 1955.

Similar to the above, though a larger proportion of the book is given to the introductory analysis of local architectural traditions. Italian towns are expertly analysed.

Smith, G. E. Kidder. *The New Architecture of Europe*. Penguin Books, 1962.

A most useful pocket guide to the various countries' achievements, with an account of a few typical buildings in each.

Smith, G. E. Kidder. *The New Churches of Europe*. London: The Architectural Press, 1964.

Whittick, Arnold. *Eric Mendelsohn*. London: Faber and Faber, 1940.

On the work of this eminent architect who was famous in Germany before the Nazi regime and afterwards worked in this country, in Palestine, and in the U.S.A. The text is rather uncritical but the book includes a good summary of the early history of modern architecture in Germany and elsewhere.

Yorke, F. R. S. *The Modern House*. London: The Architectural Press, 1934 (since revised and brought up to date).

An important book historically: the first collection of illustrations of the new domestic architecture presented to the English public.

Yorke, F. R. S. *The Modern House in England*. London: The Architectural Press, 1937 (since revised).

A sequel to the above. It is notable that during only three years after the first of these two books was published so many modern houses were built in England that it was possible to publish a second one containing none but English examples, of which the first included only half a dozen.

Zevi, Bruno. *Towards an Organic Architecture*. London: Faber and Faber, 1950.

Translation of a book by an Italian critic who is an enthusiastic admirer of Frank Lloyd Wright, and makes a somewhat incoherent attack on the more doctrinaire modernists.

3. Town Planning

Cullen, Gordon. *Townscape*. London: The Architectural Press, 1961.

An original and revealing analysis of the visual values in town design.

Gibberd, Frederick. *Town Design*. London: The Architectural Press, 1953.

An exhaustively illustrated study of the relations between buildings, with examples drawn from all countries and all centuries.

Howard, Ebenezer. *Garden Cities of To-morrow*. London: Faber and Faber, 1946.

A reprint of a celebrated book first published in 1898, which has had a profound influence all over the world. Its main proposals still apply today.

Korn, Arthur. *History Builds the Town*. London: Lund Humphries, 1954.

What its title suggests; historical and sociological in treatment, but throwing much light on the nature of present-day cities.

Le Corbusier. *Concerning Town-Planning*. London: The Architectural Press, 1947.

A translation of the French master's first post-war book. A characteristically stimulating mixture of shrewd criticism and wild generalization, with the author's own sketches.

Le Corbusier. *La Ville Radieuse*. Boulogne: 'L'Architecture d'Aujour d'hui', 1935.

Le Corbusier's famous project for a Utopian planned city.

Mumford, Lewis. *The Culture of Cities*. London: Secker and Warburg, 1938.

An encyclopedic study of the part cities have played in the history of humanity, including a forecast of the future form of the city.

Sert, J. L. *Can our Cities Survive?* Harvard University Press: Oxford University Press, 1942.

The results of researches by various European architects into city planning problems.

BIBLIOGRAPHY

Sharp, Thomas. *Town Planning*. Penguin Books, 1940.

A simple exposition, though written before much of the important English town-planning legislation.

Traffic in Towns. London: H.M. Stationary Office, 1963.

The epoch-making report of a research team under Colin Buchanan, dealing with the problem that dominates town building today.

Tunnard, Christopher. *Gardens in the Modern Landscape*. London: The Architectural Press, 1938 (since revised).

A partly historical book that leads up to a theory of garden design in keeping with the ideas of modern architects.

Tyrwhitt, J. (edited by). *The Heart of the City*. London: Lund Humphries, 1952.

Studies of town and city centres and the modern architect's and planner's approach to them, adapted from the material collected for a congress on the subject, held by C.I.A.M. in 1951. Illustrated by projects and executed schemes from many parts of the world.

4. PERIODICALS

The Architectural Review. London: The Architectural Press. Monthly.

The principal architectural magazine. In it will be found detailed illustration of new modern buildings, as well as articles on all aspects of architecture.

Architectural Design. London: Monthly.

For illustrations of new modern buildings.

The Architects' Year Book. London: Paul Elek.

A varied, but sometimes rather doctrinaire, collection of illustrations of modern buildings and articles, general and technical.

The best of the foreign architectural periodicals are *Progressive Architecture* (American), *L'Architecture d'Aujourd'hui* (French), *Domus* and *Casabella* (Italian), *Bauen und Wohnen* (German), and *Byggmästaren* (Swedish).

INDEX

INDEX

Aalto, Alvar, 85, 93, 111, 150
Acoustics, 158, 164
Adam Brothers, 20
Adler, Dankmar, 71
Air-conditioning, 31, 58
Aluminium, 57
Arch, the pointed, 30
Architects' Collaborative, 111
    Co-Partnership, 119
Aristocracy, influence of, 19, 21
Armstrong and MacManus, 118
Art Nouveau, 67–9, 74–6, 132
Arts and Crafts Movement, 63, 68,
    73–4, 82
Arup, Ove, 119
Asbestos, 57
Ashbee, C. R., 65
Aslin, C. H., 119
Asplund, Gunnar, 85, 91, 105
Azuleijos, 108, 159

Backstrom and Reinius, 151
Bassett-Lowke, house for, 76
Bauhaus, the, 81–4, 92, 133
Beardsley, Aubrey, 67
Beaudouin and Lods, 85
Bedford Park, 65
Behrens, Peter, 74–6, 133
Berlage, H. P., 70, 72–3
Berlin, Turbine factory, 76, 133
    Siedlungen near, 80–1, 133
Bessemer process, 46
Brasilia, 108, 159
Brazil, 107–8, 140, 159
Breuer, Marcel, 85–7, 96, 109, 155–6
Brinkman and Van ver Vlugt, 85
Brise-soleil, 108, 140
Brunel, I. K., 41, 67
Bunshaft, Gordon, 112

Cairns and De Mars, 113
Cantilever, 52, 54–5, 110, 137, 140
Cast iron, 46
Chamberlin, Powell and Bon, 118
Chermayeff, Serge, 147
Chicago, 70–3, 108, 110, 132, 140,
    158
    Carson Pirie Scott store, 70
    exhibition, 71
    Home Insurance building, 70
    Marshall Field store, 70
C.I.A.M., 100
Cities, growth of, 25
Clarke Hall, Denis, 119
Classes, the middle, 21–2
Coates, Wells, 85
Coignet, 47
Concrete, 32, 55, 57, 66
    pre-stressed, 48
    reinforced, 45–50, 56, 77–8, 133,
        137, 140
    shell, 48
Connell, Ward and Lucas, 85
Cost of building, 13, 45, 76, 115–16
Costa, Lucio, 107, 108
Crabtree, William, 145
Crystal Palace, the, 46, 66–7, 132
Cubism, 78–9, 84

Daguerre, 77
Davies, Richard Llewelyn, 119
Dawber, Guy, 65
De Dion, 49, 77
Department stores, 26, 145
Dessau, 81, 83, 133
De Stijl, 78
Detroit factory, 113
Doesberg, 78
Duiker, J., 85

INDEX

Eames, Charles, 112
Eesteren, van, 85
Eiffel, Gustave, 49, 132
Emberton, Joseph, 85
Engineers, 39–41, 46, 62, 65–6, 77
Exhibitions, Paris, 49, 68, 77, 132
    South Bank, 120, 161
    Stockholm, 91, 105, 137

Factories, 21, 26–7, 49, 164
Factory system, the, 31, 33, 37, 45
Farkas, Molnar, 85
Farmer and Dark, 119
Farsta, 105
Fascism, Italian, 87–8, 148
Finland, 150
Finsbury, 57, 98, 147–8
First principles, return to, 26–7, 38
Flat roof, the, 52
Flats, 25, 117, 141–3, 151–3, 161, 162, 165
Forbat, Fred, 85
Frame construction, 54–5, 146
Frank, Josef, 85
Freyssinet, Eugène, 49
Fry, Maxwell, 85
Fuchs, Bohuslav, 85
Functionalism, 11, 37, 83
Futurism, 87

Garden City, 65
Garden suburb, the first, 65
Garnier, Tony, 78
Gatwick airport, 165
Georgian architecture, 17–18, 27, 34, 42, 54, 74, 79
Germany, 57, 154, 156
Gibberd, Frederick, 117
Gibbs, James, 74
Gibson, D., 119
Glasgow School of Art, 68, 132
Glass in architecture, 57, 145–6
Gocar, Josef, 85
Goff, Bruce, 112
Goldfinger, Ernö, 119
Gollins, Melvin and Ward, 119
Goodwin, Philip, 95

Gothic architecture, 29–30, 34, 42, 55, 62–3, 104
Gothic Revival, the, 20–2, 62–3, 66, 69
Greek architecture, 30, 79
Greek Revival, the, 20–2
Green and Maybeck, 110
Gropius, Walter, 80, 82–3, 87, 96, 109, 111, 133–4, 155–6
Gruen and Krummeck, 113–14

Haefeli, 85
Halland, house at, 146–7
Harlow, 117
Harrison and Abramovitz, 112
Harrison, Wallace K., 114
Havlicek and Honzik, 85
Hawksmoor, 74
Heating, central, 31, 50
Heidelberg, college at, 154, 156
Hennebique, 47, 77
Hertfordshire schools, 118–19, 160
Hoffman, Joseph, 74, 76
Holabird and Roche, 70
Holford, W. G., 119
Hood, R., and Howells, J. M., 95
Hospitals, 26, 31
Housing, 14, 27, 115–18, 138, 161
Howard, Ebenezer, 65
Howe and Lescaze, 95, 112
Hungary, 103

Industrial buildings, 26
Industrial designer, the, 43
Industrial Revolution, the, 20–2, 62, 116
Italy, 57, 87, 105–6, 148

Japan, 108
Jenney, William Le Baron, 70
Johansen, John, 110
Johnson, Philip, 111
Johnson-Marshall, S., 119
Jordan, Robert Furneaux, 120

Kahn, Louis, 112
Kent, William, 74
Kump, E., and Co., 112

La Tourette, 106
Land, ownership of, 14
  value of, 25, 72
Landscape, architecture in the, 125–6
Lasdun, Denys, 119
Le Corbusier, 38–9, 78, 80, 83–5, 89, 100, 106–8, 114, 135–7, 140, 152–3
Lescaze, William, 85, 95
Lethaby, W. R., 65
Levassor, 77
Levi, Rino, 107
Lift, the, 58, 71
Lille, 78
Loghem, J. B. van, 85
London
  Broadcasting House, 26
  Daily Express building, 57
  Kensal House, 144
  Peter Jones store, 45, 54, 145
  Regent Street, 59
  Ritz Hotel, 45, 72
  Royal Festival Hall, 120, 163–4
  St Katharine's Dock, 131
  Selfridge's, 45, 76
  Shell-Mex House, 26
  Westminster, flats at, 161–3
London County Council, 87, 118
Loos, Adolf, 75–6
Lubetkin, B., 85
Lurçat, André, 85
Lutyens, Edwin, 65
Lyons, Eric, 119

Machinery, influence of, 22, 28, 34, 36–7, 42, 121
Machines, beauty of, 39–40
Mackintosh, C. R., 65, 68, 72, 95, 132
McKim, Mead, and White, 72
Mai, Ernst, 85
Maillart, Robert, 134–5
Malevich, 85
Markelius, Sven, 85
Marrinetti, 88
Marseilles, flats at, 107, 152–3
M.A.R.S. Group, 100
Martin, J. L., 117, 163
Mass-production, 21, 43, 66, 82

Massachusetts, houses in, 155–6
  Institute of Technology, 111
Materials, new, 30–1, 38, 45, 57, 59
Matthew, Robert, 119, 163
Mendelsohn, Erich, 85, 87, 96, 142
Mexico University, 108
Mies van de Rohe, 85, 87, 109–10, 158
Milan, Pirelli building, 148
Modernistic architecture, 11, 113, 121
Moholy-Nagy, 109
Mondrian, Piet, 79
Monier, 47
Morris, William, 35–7, 56, 63–5, 67, 73, 82, 132
Moser, Karl and Werner, 85
Muthesius, Hermann, 69

Nazi regime, the, 81, 85–7, 89, 95, 106, 142, 156
Neo-Liberty, 106
Neutra, Richard, 85, 94, 109, 157
New York, 58
  Daily News Building, 95
  Guggenheim Museum, 110
  Lever Building, 114
  Museum of Modern Art, 95, 109
  Rockefeller Centre, 95
  Seagram Building, 111
  Woolworth Building, 72
  World Fair, 93
  United Nations Building, 114
Newton, Ernest, 65
Niemeyer, Oscar, 107, 108, 159
Nineteenth-century architecture, 16, 61, 64–71, 125
Norman architecture, 30

Official architecture, 96–7
Orly, hangars at, 49, 133
Ornament, 22, 30, 35, 42, 75
Östberg, Ragnar, 92
Oud, J. J. P., 79, 84

Paris, 77–8
  school at Villejuif, 138
Paxton, Joseph, 41, 66–7, 132

Pei, I. M., 112
Penguin Pool, 144
Perret, Auguste, 77, 135
Pevsner, Nikolaus, 61, 120
Philadelphia, 95, 112
Planning, buildings, 50, 90–1, 128
    towns, 14, 25, 62, 116
Plastics, 57
Plischke, Ernst, 85
Plywood, 57–8
Poelzig, Hans, 74, 85
Poland, 103
Politics, influence of, 14, 87–90, 95,
    102
Population, 21, 25
Powell and Moya, 118, 162
Prefabrication, 32–4, 43, 67, 116–17,
    119, 132
Pugin, Augustus Welby, 62, 66

Rapson, Ralph, 112
Red House, Bexley Heath, 63, 132
Refrigeration, 31, 58
Regency stucco, 57
Reidy, Affonso, 107
Renaissance, the, 17, 34, 54, 56
Richardson, Henry Hobson, 70
Rio de Janeiro, 107, 157
Roberto, M. and M., 107
Roehampton, 118, 165
Roman architecture, 30, 37, 46
Rome, railway station, 148
Ronchamp, chapel, 107, 152
Roth, Alfred, 85
Rotterdam, flats, 138
Rudolph, Paul, 110
Ruskin, John, 63, 66
Russia, architecture in, 88–90, 102,
    103

Saarinen, Eliel; Eero, 112–113, 157
Samuely, F. J., 120
Sant' Elia, Antonio, 88
Säynätsalo, 150
Schools, 27, 98, 118–19, 138, 158,
    164
Scott, Baillie, 65
Sert, Jose Luis, 85, 109

Sezession, Viennese, 76
Shaw, Norman, 64–5, 67, 70
Sheffield, 116
Sheppard, Richard, 119
Simmons, William, 47
Skidmore, Owings, and Merrill,
    112, 114
Skyscraper, the, 58, 71, 140
Speed in building, 33
Spence, Basil, 119
Stam, Mart, 85
Standardization, 43–4, 109, 119
Steam-power, effect of, 21
Steel frame, the, 32, 45, 50, 71, 142
Steel in building, 45, 49, 55, 66, 132–3
Steiger, R., 85
Stephenson, Robert, 41, 67
Stockholm
    Crematorium, 105, 150
    Exhibition, 91, 105, 137
    flats at, 105, 151
    Town Hall, 64, 92
Stone, Edward D., 95
Strnad, Otto, 85
Stubbins, Hugh, 112
Suburbs, growth of, 25
Sullivan, Louis, 70–2, 132
Summerson, John, 120
Swedish architecture, 91–3, 105,
    150–1
Syrkus, Symon and Helena, 85

Tait, T. S., 85
Taliesin, 93, 157
Taut, Bruno, 85
Tecton, 99, 143, 149
Telford, Thomas, 41, 67, 131
Tengbom, Ivar, 92
Timber, 58
Tokyo, Imperial Hotel, 73
Townsend, C. H., 65
Transport, 14, 25, 134, 150, 165
    London, 99, 141
T.V.A., 94

U.S.A., architecture in, 19, 69, 73,
    87, 93–6, 107–14, 156–60

INDEX

Vällingby, 105
Van de Velde, Henri, 67, 69, 72, 74–5, 81
Vauban, 77
Victorian age, 16, 20, 22
Victorian architecture, 35, 52
Viollet-le-Duc, 63
Vitruvius, 37
Voysey, C. F. A., 64–5, 67, 95, 131

Wagner, Otto, 72, 74
Walpole, Horace, 20
Walton, George, 65
Webb, Philip, 63–5, 67
Weimar School, 69, 74, 81

Werkbund, Deutscher, 74–6
Williams, Owen, 85
Wren, Sir Christopher, 74
Wright, Frank Lloyd, 72–3, 84, 93–4, 100, 109–10, 133, 157
Wurster, W. W., 111

Yamasaki, Minoru, 112
Yorke, F.R.S., 85
Rosenberg and Mardall, 119
Yugoslavia, 103

Zoo buildings, 99, 144
Zurich, flats at, 139

*Some other Pelican books
are described on the
following pages*

PIONEERS OF MODERN DESIGN

Nikolaus Pevsner

The history of the Modern Movement in architecture and design was an almost unknown field until Nikolaus Pevsner first published his *Pioneers* in 1936. This soon came to be recognized as the standard work on the subject and was revised and enlarged in 1949 and has been again revised and partly rewritten for this Pelican edition. Professor Pevsner tells the exciting story of how the efforts of a relatively small group of men lifted our visual concepts away from stale Victorian Historicism and infused them once more with honesty, fitness of purpose, and contemporary expression. He shows how the foundation of the best that surrounds us today was laid then by men who thought and taught as well as designed.

Also available

AN OUTLINE OF EUROPEAN ARCHITECTURE

LE CORBUSIER

ARCHITECTURE AND FORM

Peter Blake

In the battle for honest standards in modern architecture Le Corbusier, who has been called 'the Leonardo da Vinci of our epoch', has played a unique role. Largely because of him we now regard vast blocks of reinforced concrete, balanced on slim stilts, or 'superimposed villas' as being almost the normal.

In this well-illustrated study of 'a plastic artist of supreme authority', a distinguished American architect shows how 'Corbu' has advanced his ideas almost as much in print and in plans as he has by the standing examples of the chapel at Ronchamp, the apartment block at Marseille, or the planned city of Chandigarh. He introduces us to a talented and provocative personality who, though influenced by such movements as Art Nouveau, Machine Art, and Cubism, has never diverged very far from the highroad of Mediterranean architecture.

'Should afford the lay reader a sight of Corb as he is seen by architects. . . . To read it is not only to understand better a master architect, it is to understand better all architects' – *New Statesman*

MIES VAN DER ROHE

ARCHITECTURE AND STRUCTURE

Peter Blake

Among the great personalities who have pioneered this century's revolution in building, Mies van der Rohe, for twenty years director of architecture at the Illinois Institute of Technology, is the least theoretical, the most practical, and in many ways the most inspired. The son of a simple mason in Germany, he served an apprenticeship amid the dirt and noise of building sites. He comprehends materials perfectly, from the modest brick to the marble and onyx of his famous Barcelona Pavilion or the expanses of glass on the magnificent bronze-tinted Seagram Building in New York. For him structure is an overriding principle.

'I don't want to be interesting,' he once stated. 'I want to be good.' Nevertheless it is impossible not to be interested by the career of this most professional of architects, with his severe classical standards and his ability to throw off such intriguing principles as 'Less is more'.

This study by a distinguished American architect is taken from *The Master Builders*, described by Sir Herbert Read as 'a perceptive and exciting book'.

NOT FOR SALE IN THE U.S.A. OR CANADA

FRANK LLOYD WRIGHT

ARCHITECTURE AND SPACE

Peter Blake

'In this story,' as Frank Lloyd Wright once said, 'I am God.'
As the lawgiver of modern architecture, he had been compared
to Moses.

This great pioneer, who was twenty years ahead of Europe,
was perhaps the last of the true Americans. Taking his cues
from Sullivan and the skyscrapers of the Chicago School, he
introduced – with the horizontal lines of his Prairie house – a
new domestic architecture for the wide lands. With his Imperial
Hotel in Tokyo, which stood firm through the 1923 earthquake,
and later with the unorthodox Johnson Wax building, he
demonstrated an original genius for structure. In aesthetic
terms few architects have known how to interlock spaces and
masses with the kind of poetry he built into the Kaufmann
house, above its waterfall, and few have come much nearer to
'continuous, plastic structure' than Wright did, when almost
ninety, with the new Guggenheim Museum.

For a complete list of books available please write to Penguin Books
whose address can be found on the back of the title page